Long Island's Most Haunted

A Ghost Hunter's Guide

The Paranormal Adventurers:
Joseph Flammer and Diane Hill

Schiffer Publishing Ltd

4880 Lower Valley Road, Atglen, Pennsylvania 19310

_2948166_

Other Schiffer Books on Related Subjects:

Spooky Creepy Long Island, 978-0-7643-2814-5, $12.95
Ghosts of New York City, 0-7643-1714-8, $12.95
UFOs Over New York, 978-0-7643-2974-6, $16.99
Ghosts of Manhattan, 978-0-7643-3073-5, $12.99

Schiffer Books are available at special discounts for bulk purchases for sales promotions or premiums. Special editions, including personalized covers, corporate imprints, and excerpts can be created in large quantities for special needs. For more information contact the publisher:

Schiffer Publishing Ltd.
4880 Lower Valley Road
Atglen, PA 19310
Phone: (610) 593-1777; Fax: (610) 593-2002
E-mail: Info@schifferbooks.com

For the largest selection of fine reference books on this and related subjects, please visit our web site at: **www.schifferbooks.com**. We are always looking for people to write books on new and related subjects. If you have an idea for a book please contact us at the above address.

This book may be purchased from the publisher. Include $5.00 for shipping. Please try your bookstore first. You may write for a free catalog.

In Europe, Schiffer books are distributed by:

Bushwood Books
6 Marksbury Ave.
Kew Gardens
Surrey TW9 4JF England
Phone: 44 (0) 20 8392 8585; Fax: 44 (0) 20 8392 9876
E-mail: info@bushwoodbooks.co.uk
Website: www.bushwoodbooks.co.uk

Designed by Stephanie Daugherty
Type set in Grasshopper/NewsGoth BT

ISBN: 978-0-7643-3293-7
Printed in the United States of America

Acknowledgments

We wrote this book with a little help from our friends and we'd like to recognize them and our colleagues in the paranormal community who contributed personal experiences, photographs, and their investigative talents.

Most especially we wish to thank Karen Isaksen of Bay Shore, who not only contributed her talents as a sensitive and an investigator, but also used her artistic ability to render drawings for this book. We love you, Karen.

It is with deep appreciation that we thank Kathy Abrams of Bethpage, Matt Haas of Oceanside, Erica Popino of Holtsville, and Mike Salvia of Old Bethpage for their contributions to this book: your talent and dedication is invaluable to us and to Long Island's paranormal community.

Acknowledgments

We would like to acknowledge Patchogue resident Steven Gill, *The Long Island Advance's* Man of the Year for 2007. His tireless work on behalf of the Cemetery Restoration Committee in Patchogue bridges the past to the present and future. We appreciate his contributions to not only this book, but also to the world we live in. Thank you, Steve.

Laurie Farber, director of the Starflower Experience based in Sweet Hollow Hall, you have been an amazing help with your knowledge of the West Hills Nature Preserve and of the overall Sweet Hollow area and its history, which you generously shared with us. We appreciate the time and hard work you put in climbing Mt. Misery with us as our guide. We're glad you didn't get poison ivy.

We are grateful to the program directors in libraries across Nassau, Suffolk, and Queens who have given us a forum and supported our programs over the years. It's a pleasure working with you.

We would also like to acknowledge and thank our audiences. Your stories and experiences with the paranormal inspire us.

And our hats are off to the Suffolk County Police officers who stopped us many times on Sweet Hollow Road, but were nothing but kind to us — even that time we got caught hiding behind bushes during our Paranormal Undercover study.

Lastly and most importantly, to our families: Thank you for putting up with us missing soccer games, fishing trips, and family time. We thank you from the bottom of our hearts for allowing us to chase our dreams, even if they turn out — like everything else — to be illusion.

Contents

Introduction

"Is anyone home?"

There was no answer. Kathy was all alone.

The light from the television cast giant shadows on the walls. She couldn't shake the feeling she was being watched.

The young Bethpage woman muted the sound of the television with the remote and listened... She heard breathing. She got up, opened the bedroom door, and shouted, "Is someone here?"

There was no response.

"I shouldn't watch horror movies when I'm alone," she said to herself, shutting off the television.

She got into bed, but left her bedside light on low because she was too scared to sleep in the dark. Just as she was drifting off to sleep, she heard the breathing *again*.

Too scared to turn around, Kathy grabbed a hand mirror off the nightstand and positioned it so she could look over her shoulder. Reflected in the mirror she saw the partial face of a man.

She screamed, threw the mirror, and leapt out of bed... prepared to confront the intruder. But there was no one there. She was all alone.

‡‡‡‡‡‡‡‡‡

Whether it's the ghost of Mary floating down Sweet Hollow Road or confronting a phantom man who appears in your bedroom, seeing a ghost can change your life forever.

Joseph's Experience

I saw my first ghost at a creek in Oceanside, Long Island when I was fifteen, along with five other people. The white ghost—a poltergeist—floated over a creek after drawing attention to itself by creating the sounds and movements of stomping feet running alongside us...a group of VERY stunned teenagers.

Since then I realized I was being "invited" to become a ghost hunter by the ghosts themselves. My list of paranormal experiences range from spirits whispering in my ear to being slapped repeatedly while photographing ghosts on Sweet Hollow Road. Personal knowledge now compels me to pursue the paranormal. There is no looking back...I AM a ghost hunter.

Diane's Experience

My husband and I moved into a haunted house in Lake Ronkonkoma, Long Island just after we were married. We could often hear footsteps, raps, and murmurs when we were alone in the house.

One night, I was suddenly awakened from a sound sleep. Standing in my bedroom were two apparitions dressed in trench coats and hats. The ghosts were pointing at me and having an animated conversation that I could not hear.

Ghosts have always been a part of my life. I was raised in an Italian family. Seeing, hearing, and sensing the spirits of deceased loved ones was not unusual. However, the ghosts in my bedroom were not relatives. Their presence didn't frighten me, but I wondered why they appeared. Was it a subtle challenge to further explore the paranormal? I accepted the challenge and became a ghost hunter. Now, new challenges await me at each investigation.

Why Long Island?

Long Island has a rich history. It was home to Native Americans, settled by the Europeans, and occupied by British soldiers during the American Revolution. The ground holds memories...good and bad. The ghosts of Long Island's past are among us. They linger in shadows in the woods and fly across cemeteries in the night. Their murmuring voices echo along quiet country roads. These are the ghosts of people from Long Island's past—and they might not know they're dead yet.

In this ghost hunter's guide, we take you to Long Island's most active paranormal hotspots. We chose four locations that are easily accessible. These are places we've personally investigated and experienced paranormal phenomena. Perhaps the stories will inspire you to visit these places and maybe you, too, will see a ghost!

Though we have photographs throughout the book of the places we are discussing, much of the photographic evidence we'd like to share with you can be viewed online. It's a simple process that involves visiting our website at www.paranormaladventurers. com and following the easy links. The images will be clearer and can be enlarged for further study.

So come along with us as we take you to *Long Island's Most Haunted Places*...where a life-changing experience may await you.

1

Lakeview Cemetery

Location: West Main Street, Patchogue Village

Description: Lakeview Cemetery is one of five cemeteries on the corner of West Main Street and Waverly Avenue. The other four

Entrance to Lakeview Cemetery. A headless ghost was spotted wandering the graveyard following the burial of the sailors from the *Louis V. Place* shipwreck. *Photo by The Paranormal Adventurers.*

cemeteries are Rice, Old Episcopal, Union, and Gerard, but all five of them are generally referred to as Lakeview Cemetery. In all, there are approximately 1,800 graves. Visitors can drive into the cemetery by means of a long driveway from West Main Street.

How to get there: From the Long Island Expressway take exit 63 south to Main Street in Patchogue Village. Turn right onto Main Street. The cemetery is approximately a quarter of a mile west on the north side of the road.

Haunted History

Huddled in the wind off the Great South Bay is a place now noted for its ghosts.

Lakeview Cemetery, formerly known as the Episcopal Cemetery, on West Main Street has a rich history of hauntings.

There are two main ghost stories: *the doomed shipwrecks and the haunted house on Blood Hill*.

Some say the ghosts of the sailors from the *Louis V. Place* shipwreck wander the old cemetery. Others claim the ghosts are the crew from the *Nahum Chapin* shipwreck. The bodies of the sailors from both ships are buried side by side in the Sailors' Plot at Lakeview Cemetery.

In the mid 1800s, a haunted mansion stood sentinel next door to the graveyard in an area once known as "Blood Hill."

Blood Hill was so-called because of the fighting that took place there. Rough men from schooners moored in the Great South Bay would come ashore in Patchogue with pockets full of money and spend the evening drinking in taverns. Oftentimes they would get drunk and start brawls with the locals.

In 1790, Harts Tavern, which was located on land at the southwest corner of Lakeview Cemetery, played host to President

Historic sign marking the site of Hart's Tavern on infamous "Blood Hill" in Patchogue Village. *Photo by The Paranormal Adventurers.*

George Washington. During his five-day tour of Long Island, Washington stopped at Hart's Tavern to dine on fresh oysters. Today an historic sign and footstone mark the exact location of the tavern.

Seba Smith and Elizabeth Oakes-Smith occupied the elaborate mansion known as "The Willows" on Blood Hill.

Seba Smith was a well-respected writer and journalist.

His wife, Elizabeth Oakes-Smith, was a famous poet, gifted artist, and author. Folks in town thought she was eccentric because she was outspoken and actively involved in prison reform and women's rights well before it was fashionable.

Gravestones of Elizabeth Oakes-Smith and her husband Seba Smith. They once owned "The Willows" — the reputed haunted mansion on "Blood Hill" next to Lakeview Cemetery. *Photo by The Paranormal Adventurers.*

Sometimes at night the colorful couple could hear shouting and catcalls from nearby taverns.

The Smiths mysteriously abandoned the Willows in 1867. The house was finally sold in 1870.

But nobody could live there for long.

Seba Smith and Elizabeth Oakes-Smith are buried in Lakeview Cemetery in plots located about two hundred feet from where their home once stood.

Beginning in 1870, a succession of families would move into the old mansion—and then quickly move out claiming it was a horror house. Each stayed only a few days.

They all claimed to have heard screaming and moaning from a dark corner in the dungeon-like cellar, where a punishment pen for slaves had been located.

The weathered old house next to the graveyard was vacant for nearly twenty years. It was during this period that people claimed to have seen and heard strange things in and around the abandoned mansion.

During a thunderstorm, a bolt of blue lightening struck the deserted house. It caught fire. Patchogue Village residents watched the red and blue flames eat the haunted structure. They didn't try to save it.

Villagers believed the dark house was evil. They were glad to see the cursed place burn down to the ground.

Shortly after the fire, residents reported sightings of a big black ghost, dressed like a priest, wandering through the misty graveyard on rainy nights. It was said he carried a lantern with a blue flame.

‡‡‡‡‡‡‡‡‡

Shipwrecked Ghosts?

Annie and Lizzie Andreshock bolted from their howling machines in the factory as soon as the bell for the thirteenth hour tolled.

The sisters darted like fleeing prisoners through the darkened brick building, yanking on their red scarves and gloves.

The boys were sure to wave to Annie, the prettier one with the blond hair and ocean blue eyes, as the girls rushed out the main door.

Lizzie was used to being invisible when her beautiful older sister was around.

They always giggled about this after work. Annie never made Lizzie feel lesser. In fact, the sisters were best friends.

It was nine o'clock at night. Annie and Lizzie had begun their shift at eight o'clock that morning. They couldn't wait to rush into February's crisp, clean air, even if the temperature was frigid.

Breathing fresh air was always the best part of getting off the thirteenth hour shift at the stuffy Patchogue-Plymouth Lace Mill on West Main Street in Patchogue Village.

The year was 1895.

The graveyard the two young ladies had to pass on their way home from the factory had just days before been the focal point of tragedy for this waterside community. Funerals for three of the doomed sailors from the *Louis V. Place* shipwreck had been held earlier in the week.

Annie and Lizzie were no longer afraid to pass the graveyard at night even though they knew the story of the Black Ghost of Blood Hill. They heard the older folks tell of a large black ghost who wandered through Lakeview Cemetery on rainy nights carrying a blue-flamed lantern.

For months after they began working at the factory they would scurry past the foreboding graveyard, especially on rainy nights, shielding their eyes so they wouldn't catch of glimpse of the black specter.

But now the graveyard had become a familiar part of the local landscape. The sisters didn't give it much thought anymore as they walked past it on their way home from work each night. Even so, it became their habit to walk on the opposite side of the street.

With arms linked, the sisters hurried home. As they were passing just opposite the graveyard entrance on West Main Street, Annie heard an abysmal sound. She turned sharply and looked into the blackened graveyard.

What did she see that stopped her in her tracks? Grabbing Lizzie's arm, Annie pointed.

The stunned sisters watched as the form of a headless man rose like smoke from the ground at the gravesites of the recently buried sailors from the *Louis V. Place*.

Lizzie's blood-curdling scream pierced the still night air.

But Annie smiled, seemingly transfixed...

A ghostly mist forming in Lakeview Cemetery. Could this be the headless ghost seen by the Andreshock sisters in 1895? *Photo by The Paranormal Adventurers.*

The date was February 8, 1895. The doomed ship *Louis V. Place*, a three-masted schooner sailing out of Baltimore to New York, was little more than a battered iceberg in the wild and dangerous seas.

Violent weather pounded the entire East Coast. Snow slashed the sky from North Carolina all the way up to Canada. The temperature in New York City held at a steady brittle zero. Angry winds raged up to seventy-two miles an hour.

Aboard the *Louis V.* were her captain, William Squires, and seven crewmembers.

As the weather steadily worsened, Captain Squires ordered the crew to dress in layers of clothing and gave them grog to drink in an effort to keep warm as they fought to lower the sails. But the frozen sails would not budge.

The *Louis V. Place* ran aground on a sandbar four hundred yards off Fire Island across from Patchogue.

The *Louis V. Place* shipwreck, 1895.
Photo by Martin Anderson. Courtesy of Long Island Maritime Museum.

Smashing seas combed over every inch of her hull, obliterating her icy deck, sending the captain and his crew flying to the rigging for their lives.

One by one the men began to lose their battle with Mother Nature. Captain Squires was the first to fall from the rigging and was swallowed up by the raging sea. John Horton, the cook, soon followed.

Now there were six men left to do battle with the elements.

Shrieking winds and numbing cold became the survivors' constant opponents.

As night shrouded the battered ship, Charles Allen could fight no longer and he let go of the rigging, falling to his death. A short time later, Lars Gioby died from exposure and followed his shipmates into the unforgiving sea.

During the night, the storm claimed its fifth victim. In the early morning light, the frozen corpse of Felix Mard was seen swinging upside down high above the deck of the ship from the very rope he used to secure himself to the rigging. Back and forth he swung, like the pendulum of a surreal clock, counting out the seconds for the terrified sailors who remained.

Now there were three.

Soren Nelson and Claus Stuvens managed to find shelter from the savage winds by crawling into a furled topsail.

Gustaf Olsen could not reach the shelter of the canvas, so he, too, died—frozen in the rigging.

Forty hours after it first ran aground, rescue crews from the U.S. Lifesaving Service at Lone Hill across from Sayville on Fire Island were finally able to reach the ill-fated schooner.

Only Soren Nelson and Claus Stuvens survived the horrible ordeal.

Nelson died from tetanus in a hospital on Staten Island less than a month after his rescue, leaving Claus Stuvens as the lone survivor.

According to some sources, Stuvens eventually went mad and died in a mental institution in Central Islip.

Man frozen in the rigging of the *Louis V. Place*.
Photo by Martin Anderson. Courtesy of Long Island Maritime Museum.

Frozen remains of the *Louis V. Place*.
Photo by Martin Anderson. *Courtesy of Long Island Maritime Museum.*

The lifesaving crew went back to the ship the next day to retrieve the bodies of the men frozen in the rigging.

During the ordeal, nearly 1,000 people gathered on the beach at Fire Island to watch the tragedy unfold. Most of the spectators either walked or drove in horse-drawn sleighs over the frozen Great South Bay from villages and hamlets dotting Long Island's south shore.

Some curious onlookers reported seeing the ghostly image of Captain Squires appear in the rigging of the doomed schooner.

A photograph of the captain's ghostly image is displayed as part of the *Louis V. Place* exhibit at the Long Island Maritime Museum in West Sayville.

The captain was the first man to fall into the churning sea from the *Louis V. Place*. Were the people who saw the captain's ghost in the rigging imagining it or did the image appear because of the time-honored tradition that the captain goes down with his ship?

In December 1924, crewmembers of the *S.S. Watertown* had a similar experience. The ship, a large oil tanker, was heading to Panama from the United States.

Two men cleaning one of the tanks were overcome by fumes and died. Both were buried at sea.

The following day members of the crew reported seeing images of the two men floating next to the ship. They appeared and disappeared, but kept pace with the ship's journey. Every man on the ship eventually witnessed the floating images.

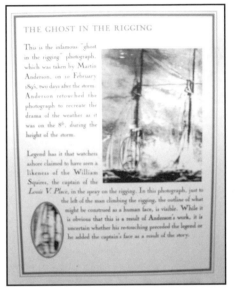

Ghost in the Rigging part of the *Louis V. Place* Exhibit at the Long Island Maritime Museum in West Sayville. Do you see the ghost of Captain Squires in the rigging? *Photo by The Paranormal Adventurers.*

When the captain of the *Watertown* reported the phenomenon to the company's officials, he was told to buy a camera and take photographs of the faces in the water the next time they were spotted.

The captain took six photographs and then locked the camera in a safe. When the ship pulled into port, the safe was opened and the camera went directly to a developer.

One photograph clearly showed the ghostly images of the dead shipmates. As expected, neither the photograph nor the negative showed any signs of tampering.

Thirteen days after the *Louis V. Place* shipwrecked, the captain's body washed ashore in Hampton Bays, which was then known as Good Ground.

Captain Squires was known to be a dedicated family man who loved his home.

Gravesites of Captain Squires and his family, Good Ground Cemetery in Hampton Bays. *Photo by The Paranormal Adventurers.*

So...was it coincidence or a paranormal event that his body drifted thirty miles against the tide to reach his birthplace? Even death could not stop Captain Squires from returning home from the sea.

The bodies of Olsen and Mard, who died in the rigging, and Gioby, whose body had washed ashore at Forge River Station on Fire Island across from Mastic, were taken to C. W. Ruland Funeral Home in Patchogue Village.

The Patchogue Advance reported that week, "The bodies presented a horrible sight and scores of people to satisfy their morbid curiosity went to Ruland's undertaking rooms to see them."

From there the bodies were buried in Lakeview Cemetery. Generous Patchogue resident Augusta Weeks donated the plots.

In some accounts of the *Louis V. Place* shipwreck, the cook has been identified as Charles Morrison. However, in e-mails exchanged with Bradley Sheard, author of *Lost Voyages: Two Centuries of Shipwrecks in the Approaches to New York*, Sheard

Gravesites and memorial gravestones for the sailors of the *Louis V. Place*. Plots were donated by Augusta Weeks. *Courtesy of Long Island Maritime Museum.*

stated that Harry Squires, the only son of Captain William Squires, identified the cook as John J. Horton, the name etched on the memorial gravestone in Lakeview Cemetery. Horton's was the only body never recovered.

‡‡‡‡‡‡‡‡‡

Lizzie's eyes widened in horror as the figure began moving. The headless white ghoul was making its way toward them.

She yanked on her sister's sleeve. "Run Annie!" she shouted.

But Annie did not move. She was frozen in place as she watched the creature advancing toward them like a beheaded soldier in search of his head.

Hypnotized, Annie stepped off the curb towards the ghost.

Lizzie gasped. "Annie!" she shrieked in a high voice. "What are you doing?"

Annie seemed momentarily dazed. She turned to her sister. Seeing the fear in Lizzie's eyes woke her up. She jerked forward as though someone was about to grab her shoulder...but the ghost was still in the graveyard.

With her heart pounding loudly in her ears, Lizzie grabbed Annie's hand and pulled her back up onto the sidewalk. She had to get away from the graveyard.

Annie looked over her shoulder as the girls fled down the street. The ghost was no longer moving. The headless apparition was sitting in front of a tree where the reputed haunted house on Blood Hill once stood. She yanked Lizzie hand, forcing her to stop.

"Look Lizzie. He's just sitting there," Annie said. She caught sight of her sister's frightened face. "There is nothing to be afraid of. He's not coming after us," Annie reassured her.

But Lizzie was scared. "I don't care!" she cried. "I want to go home!"

Just before they reached their front door, Annie stopped and faced her sister. "Lizzie," she said solemnly, "we saw death tonight."

Lizzie closed her eyes and whispered, "I know."

‡‡‡‡‡‡‡‡‡

The Brooklyn Daily Eagle, a prominent New York newspaper at the time, reported the following:

Patchogue L.I. – "This village has a new ghost which appears every night in the Episcopal Cemetery about a quarter mile from the center of town. The apparition has aroused the curiosity and fears of the people in the section of the village where the cemetery is located. Children do not venture out after dark and quite a number of adults are loathe to pass by the cemetery.

Those who have doubted the story have been thoroughly convinced of the fact that something unusual is going on after a visit there."

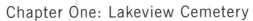

According to the newspaper, the figure "...rises slowly from the ground. It hesitates for a second and then proceeds toward the road."

The story goes on to say: "After going a few steps it suddenly turns and starts for the edge of the cemetery where it halts against a tree upon the spot where an alleged haunted house once stood."

‡‡‡‡‡‡‡‡‡‡

Arriving at work the next morning, Annie and Lizzie, still shaken from their haunting experience, told their friends, Lizzie and Bertie Hassler and Lizzie Grundy, about what they had seen. Their friends snickered at the outlandish story and told the girls they were probably dreaming.

That evening the Hassler sisters and Lizzie Grundy were returning from work.

The three girls were talking about the absurd ghost story as they approached the graveyard. They stopped in front of it. Two of the girls threw their hands in the air and began making ghostly sounds as they circled the third girl. Gales of laughter echoed throughout the quiet street.

Suddenly, their laughter turned to terrified shrieks—as a headless white ghost staggered through the dark graveyard towards the road!

The girls stood rooted to the spot in front of the cemetery gates clutching each other's hands. As the headless figure staggered closer, the girls heard its low mournful cries.

Bertie Hassler, standing between her sister and Lizzie Grundy, snatched their hands and yanked them into the street and away from the graveyard gate.

The trio took off running and did not stop until they reached home.

The Andreshock sisters weren't dreaming. The ghost was real!

‡‡‡‡‡‡‡‡‡‡

Communicating with the "Other Side"

There was just a sliver of moon on this clear, cold winter's night. Patchogue was a ghost town. Though it was only 9:30 in the evening it seemed nobody was out tonight. West Main Street was deserted.

Joe and I drove to Patchogue because we planned on taking some photographs of Lakeview Cemetery from the street. We were hoping to catch the wandering graveyard ghost.

We wanted the same vantage point as the Andreshock sisters and their friends when they witnessed the headless white specter while on their way home from the lace mill that February in 1895.

Whenever we visit the cemetery, it's our habit to drive onto the property over the rutted, uneven road past the stark white headstones that mark the graves of the Sailors' Plot. The plot includes the graves of the sailors from the *Louis V. Place* and the *Nahum Chapin* shipwrecks. But on this night I parked on West Main Street directly across from the cemetery entrance.

Joe got out of my black Saturn VUE and went to the back to get some camera equipment. He slammed the hatch and admonished me to lock the doors. I did.

I watched Joe walk across the street. He stood before the rusted black wrought iron fence that surrounds the graveyard and began photographing.

Normally, I take advantage of this time alone to return phone calls. This night, however, I felt the need to relax and be a spectator.

Glancing into the graveyard I could see a long line of white headstones illuminate each time Joe took a photograph. These were the graves of the Sailors' Plot. I strained my eyes to see if I could detect any ghostly images in the camera's bright flash. I didn't.

Impulsively I asked, "If there are any spirits in the car with me, please show me a sign of your presence?"

It's an experiment I conduct from time to time when I'm by myself — ever since we brought home the spirit of "Dorothy" from a graveyard.

People who attend our lectures always ask if it's possible to bring a spirit home from a haunted site. Our answer is always yes.

We had finished an investigation at St. George's Cemetery in Hempstead in 2005 and returned to the car. Joe said he felt as though someone was sitting beside him in the backseat. He took a few random photographs because he could not shake the feeling that we were not alone.

When we got home and downloaded the photographs, we saw that Joe had captured the image of an older woman in the side view mirror.

Now, as I sat alone in my car, just moments after my request for spirit communication, I *heard* two distinct raps coming from the back of my VUE.

"BOOM! BOOM!"

I quickly checked the backseat to see if anyone was in the car with me. When I saw I was alone, I looked to see if anyone was passing by on the street that could have been knocking on the car. But except for Joe, West Main Street was empty.

I asked, "Please rap again if there is really a spirit present."

Almost before I finished the sentence, two more raps sounded from the back of the vehicle.

Ironically, it was *rapping* that the Fox sisters heard in their home in Hydesville, New York, in 1848 that led to a movement known as **Spiritualism**.

The core belief of Spiritualism is that there is no death. The experience we call "death" is just a shedding of the body. Once free of its earthly bonds, the spirit soars and lives on...and can *communicate* from the other side.

In the case of the Fox sisters, it was the spirit of a peddler who had been murdered by a former tenant and buried in the cellar of their rented house that caused the raps.

Joe and I were well acquainted with paranormal **rapping**.

We heard raps in Stockbridge, Massachusetts in our room at the Red Lion Inn. Room 301 is the Inn's most haunted room. The management of the Inn had invited us there to investigate one weekend in March 2007.

During our investigation, our video camera, set on infrared, was focused on an area around the room's armoire because we detected a cold spot directly in front of it and our dowsing rods had been crossing at the exact spot all night. In addition, the armoire's door slowly opened by itself right in front of us and the video camera caught a mist in one of the room's mirrors.

During the course of the night, the video camera's audio caught a series of raps along with whispers and moans. While I slept, Joe heard the raps and moans as he sat in a chair in the corner of the room photographing.

The raps came in sets of two, and in one case, a set of three.

We recorded seventeen distinct sets of raps, and later, as we slept, something moved inside the room and banged into our video camera. We weren't surprised because there had been reports of a ghostly image of a man standing at the foot of the bed in front of the armoire.

So when I heard the raps as I sat alone in my car, the sound was very familiar. Wanting further validation, I requested to hear the raps a third time. As if on cue, two more raps sounded.

My body trembled with excitement. I was experiencing something every ghost investigator dreams of — a spirit was *communicating* with me! It was exhilarating!

Putting my hands together I bowed my head in a gesture of thanks to the spirit. I said out loud, "I am so grateful to you. Thank you for this unforgettable experience."

Joe returned to the car. After stowing the camera equipment in the back, he climbed into the passenger seat. He took one look at my face and asked, "What's wrong?"

I hadn't realized that I was crying.

"Are you okay?" His voice was full of concern.

Smiling, I answered, "Something incredible happened to me!"

‡‡‡‡‡‡‡‡‡‡

More people claimed to have seen the headless apparition in the graveyard on West Main Street after *The Brooklyn Daily Eagle* reported the Andreshock sisters' experience. Like the Andreshock sisters and their friends, all the witnesses reported the apparition was slim and about five feet tall.

Every night people walking by would peer into the darkened graveyard, hoping to catch a glimpse of the mysterious spirit.

Frightened wives buried their faces in their husbands' shoulders and peeked fearfully with one eye as they walked past the haunted graveyard.

Swaggering young men gathered in front of the cemetery, challenging the spirit to show itself. They were hoping to impress the pretty girls with their daring.

Children squeezed their eyes shut and hid behind their mothers' skirts so the ghost would not see them.

But this quintessential hometown ghost story was about to take a bizarre twist.

Nearly three weeks after his shipmates were buried another sailor from the *Louis V. Place* shipwreck finally washed ashore. His frozen corpse was laid to rest beside the three other sailors in Lakeview Cemetery.

That evening, a larger than normal crowd gathered outside the graveyard. Most went home cold and disappointed because the graveyard ghost did not make an appearance.

However, according to *The Brooklyn Daily Eagle*, "those who passed the stream of water just east of the graveyard at 10:30 p.m. could have seen the ghost gliding up and down the icy waters of the stream."

A local Patchogue resident, Clarence Gerard, was determined to "catch" the elusive spirit that was haunting the graveyard.

Gerard and two friends kept a close eye on the white specter. The ghost did not leave the stream until midnight.

This was the chance Gerard had been hoping for.

The newspaper reported, "The ghost had hardly shaken the water from its robes when Gerard started after it with the speed of a hound."

The ghost headed for the cemetery with Gerard and his two friends in pursuit. Only Gerard followed the ghost when it veered into the graveyard. He shouted, but the headless white specter ignored him. It deftly ran through the graveyard without tripping over gravestones and smacking headlong into trees.

Gerard chased the ghost deeper into the dark burial ground. According to *The Brooklyn Daily Eagle*, "he was fast gaining on the ghost when the specter made a bolt for Waverly Avenue." It goes on to say that, "had the ghost continued to run dressed in its white robe it would have been captured in five more minutes."

However, as the ghost bounded down Waverly Avenue, it threw off its robe and the robe "fell upon Gerard." Unencumbered, the ghost was now easily able to sprint away from its pursuer.

Gerard inspected the discarded robe. According to the newspaper reports it was made of muslin. There were sleeves for arms, but no hole for a head to go through. The piece of wood that was found with the robe evidently rested on the head to give the impression that the ghost was headless.

The Brooklyn Daily Eagle reported, "The identity of the man who played the ghost is believed to be known. Several complaints have been made against a certain man of late, and he is believed to be the man who frightened several women at Lakeview Heights."

In a subsequent issue, the newspaper stated:

"Following close upon the discovery of a ghost in the Episcopal Cemetery in Lake View Heights and its pursuit by Mr. Gerard resulting in its identification as a human being comes a big, burly negro who chases women and children in the neighborhood of the Heights. The negro has been appearing in this vicinity for the past few nights."

The suspected man was brought in for questioning. He denied any knowledge of the incidents and was eventually released. No charges were ever brought against him and no other arrests were made.

Now, this story would neatly debunk the ghost of Lakeview Cemetery if not for several glaring inconsistencies:

† The people who reported seeing the ghost stated it was *slim* and *small* in stature. Unless he was walking around on his knees the "big, burly" man the newspaper mentioned could not be the ghost.

† The newspaper stated the ghost was in an "icy stream" for nearly two hours. How, then, could someone in a wet, ice encrusted robe with frozen feet manage to outrun his pursuer who was reported in the newspaper to be "as fast as a hound"?

† It was also reported that the ghost entered the dark graveyard and ran around trees and gravestones while wearing a robe with no eyeholes and balancing a board on his head. How could he have run so easily through the graveyard while being chased and not once have fallen over a gravestone or run into a tree?

In reading this news story over carefully and objectively, we concluded that Mr. Clarence Gerard and the reporter were probably friends and maybe drinking companions. Perhaps Mr. Gerard wanted

to impress a certain young lady, and his reporter friend complied by writing the newspaper story featuring Mr. Gerard as the hero.

The only thing this story proves is that you can't always believe what you read in the newspaper.

‡‡‡‡‡‡‡‡‡

Ghost sightings at Lakeview Cemetery continued for years after the sailors from the *Louis V. Place* shipwreck were buried. But the Grim Reaper was not done with Patchogue yet.

The *Nahum Chapin*, a three-masted schooner, sealed its dark fate when it left Baltimore en route to Boston with a full load of coal just as a deadly storm was taking shape over the northeast.

It was January 21, 1897, and this killer storm was about to blow death into the village one more time.

On board Captain Ernest Arey's doomed wooden vessel were his young daughter, his dear wife, and eight members of his faithful crew.

Along the lonely beach a solitary surfman from the U.S. Life Saving Service at Quogue struggled to climb over the dunes in the freezing winter sleet and rain to better see the ghostly lights he thought he spotted just offshore. It was 4 o'clock in the morning and the stormy sky was dark and foreboding.

Sleet pelted his rugged face causing him to squint over the mountainous black waves. Ocean spray formed mist that froze on his thick eyebrows and bushy beard and slid down his yellow storm suit.

"Good God!" he exclaimed into the wild winds. "There's a ship stranded out there!"

The hearty surfman pushed through the fierce gales that sent sand swirling into his eyes and mouth as he made his way back to the life saving station to alert the men. He knew they'd be gathered around the potbellied stove of the red house station, drinking coffee out of tin cups in the dim light and trying to keep warm on this frigid night.

Bursting through the door he shouted in a whaler's New England accent, "We've got one men! She's six hundred yards off shore on the sandbar!"

The life saving crew, strong men with weathered faces, sprung into action. Tossing aside their half-filled tin cups, they yanked on their storm suits and swiftly rolled the equipment out of the red house. As they headed to the beach, they prayed they would get there in time. These hardened men had responded to emergencies like this one many times before, but it was never easy knowing people could die on *their* watch.

Pelting rain and punishing winds pummeled the lifesavers and hampered their progress as they wheeled the Lyle gun onto the beach.

Once they were across from the foundering ship, flares were fired and a bonfire was lit on shore to signal to the stranded men of the *Nahum Chapin* that help was on the way.

The life saving crew attempted to reach the distressed vessel with the Lyle gun, a cannon-like piece of equipment that launched a missile with a rope attached.

The men on shore could see the launches were successful, but it appeared no one on board the disabled schooner could reach the lines. They were too weakened and numb from the cold.

As dawn streaked across the night sky, onlookers from the mainland of Long Island gathered on the windswept beach. They could see men lashed to the frozen rigging and clinging to the jib boom of the shipwreck.

Suddenly, a huge wave hit the stranded ship with such force that the men clinging to the rigging plunged into the raging sea.

One lifesaver reported seeing a woman in a white nightgown clinging to a man. Between them there appeared to be a child. They were all flung from their precarious perch after the first wave hit.

Soon, another massive wave slammed into the wrecked schooner and sent four more men flying into the churning abyss.

Relentless waves tossed and pounded the schooner until the spars snapped and fell like dominoes crashing into the jib boom.

As the spectators on shore watched in horror, the three remaining crewmen were thrown like rag dolls into the black sea.

All aboard the *Nahum Chapin* were lost as the angry sea smashed the wooden vessel to pieces. Only five bodies were recovered.

The captain's body was the first to wash ashore. His battered corpse was returned to his home state for burial. The bodies of his wife and child were never recovered.

The waves delivered a woman's silver hairbrush, a doll, and a child-sized chair onto the beach. This was all that was left of the captain's family.

Four more bodies washed ashore, but three of them were too mutilated to be identified. They were buried in Lakeview Cemetery alongside the sailors from the *Louis V. Place* shipwreck.

The long row of white gravestones from both shipwrecks is now known as the Sailors' Plot.

Is it possible that ghosts from the crew of the *Nahum Chapin* are haunting Lakeview Cemetery along with their fellow sailors from the *Louis V. Place*?

The Sailors' Plot, final resting place and memorials for the men of the *Louis V. Place* and *Nahum Chapin* shipwrecks. *Photo by The Paranormal Adventurers.*

Blood Hill

Joe and I went in search of the haunted house on Blood Hill next to Lakeview Cemetery. There is no "hill" anymore. The land is flat.

We went through an opening in the fence between the cemetery and the overgrown lot. Brown leaves crunched beneath our boots as we fought our way through the bushes and low hanging brown branches of straggly trees. We were careful to step over the endless vines that booby-trapped our path. There were beer bottles, soda cans, and other debris indicating the lot was now a hangout place.

We heard water trickling. Following the sound we located the remains of the haunted creek where the ghost of Lakeview Cemetery was observed gliding back and forth. Nearby there was a deep gully in the ground. Inside the gully were faded red bricks and some still in old mortar, which were the remains of a chimney. The chimney belonged to the haunted mansion on Blood Hill.

The air around us felt thick and heavy. I immediately felt a chill run down my spine. I looked at Joe. By the expression on his face, I could tell he was feeling something, too. He was gazing down at the scattered bricks. No doubt he was imagining the fear felt by the slaves who were locked in the pen awaiting their owner's cruel whip.

My chest felt tight. I was finding it hard to breathe. It was similar to the feeling I sometimes get on Sweet Hollow Road in Melville when spirits are around. I wasn't frightened, but I was definitely uncomfortable.

I looked down again. In my head, I heard the echoes of moans and agonized screams. My skin felt clammy and the hair on the back of my neck stood up. I closed my eyes and tried to steady myself by taking deep breaths.

"Di, are you okay?" Joe asked. "You're as white as a ghost!"

I opened my eyes and tried to focus. "I'm getting such a creepy feeling here...I can almost smell the fear," I answered.

"I know," he replied. "I feel it, too."

I pulled my camera out of the case; I was anxious to start taking pictures. The sooner I took the photographs, the sooner we could leave this place. I aimed my camera and pressed the button. Nothing happened. I tried again: still nothing.

"Do you have extra batteries with you?" Joe asked.

"I do, but I put new ones in before we left the house," I said. I dug around in the camera bag and found an unopened package of Duracell batteries. I opened the camera and inserted four brand new batteries.

I pointed the camera again and pressed the button. It still would not work. The camera was dead.

Joe had no problem using the video camera. I stood silently while he panned the area.

The sun was going down quickly. We wanted to leave before darkness descended. We carefully made our way through the overgrown lot and back into the cemetery.

The fading light cast an orange glow over the graveyard. I thought it would make a great photograph.

I took out my camera and snapped a picture. It was working fine now. I wasn't surprised. As often happens in haunted locations, electronics sometimes fail to work properly. I've always felt it was the spirits' way of letting us know they did not want to be photographed.

I looked over at Joe and said, "Something or someone didn't want me to take any photos back there."

Joe replied, "You might be right about that. But at least that oppressive, heavy feeling we felt back inside the woods has disappeared."

"You know," I said, "we didn't recite our entreaty back there."

Before conducting any investigation in graveyards or any supposed haunted locations, we typically recite an entreaty to let the spirits know we mean them no harm and that we come in peace. We failed to do that at the site of the old mansion.

"The spirits didn't know our intention," I continued. "Maybe the black ghost with the blue-flamed lantern protects the spirits of the slaves. And maybe that's why my camera didn't work."

"That might explain it," Joe answered.

I took a few photographs of the orange sun lighting the graveyard as we made our way back to the car. It was like a fireball in the sky. I stopped to take another photograph. It was then I saw a plain gravestone with only a name, date, and age. Helen Tiernan died on May 16, 1937. She was just seven-years-old. Freshly planted mums and a little angel adorned the gravesite.

Friends of the Dead

The body of young Helen Tiernan was discovered in thick underbrush in Patchogue. Her throat had been slashed and her body hacked. The tiny girl was then tossed into a bonfire.

Helen's younger brother, James, was found nearby. He had been similarly mutilated, but was still alive when the police found him. His delirious mutterings gave police cause to suspect the murderous slasher was the children's own mother, Helen — the same name she gave the little girl she so brutally slaughtered.

According to newspaper reports, Helen Tiernan was arrested and taken to the Riverhead jail.

She went to trial for the murder of her seven-year-old daughter. In order to escape the electric chair, she pled guilty to second-degree murder. The mandatory sentence was twenty years to life.

We first learned of this grizzly murder and its visceral details from Steven C. Gill, chairman of the Cemetery Restoration Committee of Patchogue.

Gill led us to the little girl's grave, where he went to water the fall mums planted by his sister whom he said was deeply moved by Helen Tiernan's horrific story.

Later, during our conversation, Joe casually asked if Gill had ever seen a ghost in the cemetery. He laughed and said no. But then grew more serious.

"There was something," he recalled. "I saw an old man dressed in all white one Sunday in June while I was here working. He was wearing a white shirt, white pants, white suspenders, and

Steven Gill, Chairman of the Cemetery Restoration Committee of Patchogue, watering flowers planted on the grave of Helen Tiernan, age seven, who was savagely murdered and thrown in a bonfire by her mother in 1937. *Photo by The Paranormal Adventurers.*

a white hat. His hair was white and he had a long white beard like Santa Claus."

Gill went on to say he'd been weed whacking around the graves of the sailors from the *Louis V. Place* when the man in white appeared behind him. He was startled, but the old man smiled at him.

"He was a magnificent looking man," Gill stated. "We shook hands. He was extremely strong. He spoke a language I never heard before. I asked him if he lived around here and he waved his arms over the Sailors' graves."

After the exchange, Gill returned to his weed whacking. "I was nervous. He made me nervous. A minute later I turned back to see where he was and he was gone."

"Do you think he was a ghost?" Joe asked.

"No, probably not," Gill replied.

"Do you think he was an angel?" Joe asked.

37

"I don't know," Gill responded, "but I definitely think he was someone special."

Gill, who said he is a descendent of the local Swezey family, spends countless hours of his own time working to restore broken and fallen gravestones and improving Lakeview Cemetery in an effort to preserve the dignity of the dead.

One of the accomplishments of the Cemetery Restoration Committee has been to photo document each of the approximately 1,800 graves that comprise the five original graveyards that are now generally known as Lakeview Cemetery.

The motto of this forward-thinking committee is: "Restoring the past for the future!"

For his dedication and tireless effort to restore and beautify the cemeteries, *The Long Island Advance* honored Gill as "Man of the Year 2007."

In the January 4, 2008 issue — the same issue in which Gill was honored — Joe and I published a story about the Louis V. Place shipwreck and the subsequent burials at Lakeview Cemetery. The title of the story is, "Who's buried in John J. Horton's Grave?"

Gill had another strange experience, but this time he wasn't alone. He and a friend were waiting for a contractor in the cemetery early one evening. An old car from the 1930s drove up. The driver hopped out and opened the car's hood. It was a technique used by drivers long ago to cool off a car's engine.

Two women and another man emerged from the old vehicle. Gill said the two young couples were dressed in 1930s style clothing.

The couples approached him and asked if they could walk around the cemetery.

Gill responded, "Of course."

With that the group strolled off into the old section of the graveyard toward Waverly Avenue and "disappeared into the darkness," Gill said.

Gill and his friend looked at each other in amazement. His friend said, "This is too weird. Let's go home."

And they did.

Mists & Light Anomalies

So many stories pertaining to Lakeview Cemetery are from first-hand accounts by people who experienced a paranormal event within the cemetery's wrought iron fence.

It was a cold winter's evening when Joe and I were joined at Lakeview Cemetery by sensitive and paranormal investigator Karen Isaksen of Bay Shore and Erica Popino, a paranormal investigator from Holtsville.

We often invited Karen and Erica to join us on investigations when we needed additional expert skills.

Karen has an innate ability to sense the presence of spirits. She explains:

Ghostly mist traveling through Lakeview Cemetery.
Photo by The Paranormal Adventurers.

"I feel a magnetic pulling of my entire body that draws me to the area or spot of the presence or being. Occasionally I'll feel nausea or dizziness. Sometimes I may pick up the emotions of the spirit."

Her ultimate goal is to help spirits who are earthbound to go "to the light."

Erica, on the other hand, has been gifted with the ability to see spirit manifestations even when others cannot.

They were both part of our team when *Newsday* accompanied us as we conducted an investigation at a haunted house in Freeport. The house belongs to Daniel and Nancy Akner. Daniel is a well-known Long Island psychic medium and a talented artist.

Akner told us he and his wife purchased the house "because it was haunted." He said they looked at over one hundred houses before they bought this beautiful old Victorian that was once owned by a ship's captain.

According to Akner, a ghost named Rose dwells in the house. She's claimed a chair in the home's sitting room as her own and does not like anyone else to sit there. Even the cat avoids that chair.

In Lakeview Cemetery, Karen and Erica had a new challenge before them. Rather then talking to spirits in a known haunted house, we asked them to reach the spirits in this cold, dark graveyard.

Joe and I have investigated many graveyards. We've had a variety of paranormal experiences, both together and apart.

While Joe was a reporter for *The Long Island Advance*, he spent the night alone in a graveyard beside the Patchogue River for a Halloween story he was writing. The cemetery was closed for the night. He had to climb over a tall fence to get inside.

He was well prepared with blankets, food, and hot coffee in a thermos. However, most of his supplies were left behind in his haste to escape the graveyard when the night came alive with paranormal activity only a few hours after he arrived.

It was 3 o'clock in the morning. A rectangle of deep purple light suddenly emanated from a grave about a hundred feet away from where Joe was walking in the shadowy graveyard.

As he drew closer, he saw that the purple light formed a perfectly geometrical rectangle with sharp right-angled corners and straight lines. The purple light was shooting out of the ground the way light flares out from a movie projector.

Creeping closer to the grave, he switched on his brand new heavy-duty yellow flashlight. It worked before he entered the cemetery, but now when he pressed the button nothing happened. He shook the flashlight, but it still refused to work.

Rustling noises from nearby bushes alerted Joe to the fact he was not alone. At first he thought the noises might be raccoons. He paused and listened carefully. It sounded more like a human shuffling slowly toward him through dead brown leaves. The footsteps seemed to be leading up to the graveyard from the river. While he thought perhaps it might be transients who lived down by the river, the purple light beaming out of the grave told him differently. It was shooting out of the ground like a lightshow of the dead.

The air was suddenly charged with static electricity. Joe felt as though spider webs were brushing his face. Simultaneously, noises erupted all around him. His body went into a high alert mode. His brain sent out a "red alarm" code. Something terrifying was taking place.

Dropping the flashlight, he backed away from the grave that beamed the queer purple light.

He was caught in the grips of a paranormal event—an event so extraordinary he prayed he would never experience the likes of it again. With his heart pounding in his chest, he bolted across the expanse of the night-shrouded graveyard to the tall fence. His breath came in short gasps and beads of sweat broke on his face as he heaved himself over the high fence. He was desperate to get of out of there before he came face-to-face with the ghosts that surrounded him.

This (blue) orb appeared to author Diane Hill and Erica Popino during a ghost investigation at Lakeview Cemetery. The ghost of the graveyard was said to have carried a blue-flamed lantern. *Photo by The Paranormal Adventurers.*

Now, on this night years later at Lakeview Cemetery, we hoped Karen and Erica could help us reach the spirits. Joe's fear of the paranormal had long ago abated. Over the years he lost his fear of ghosts, thanks to his growing experience as a ghost investigator. He now welcomed communication with the spirits. If ghosts appeared now, Joe would not run.

A blue orb caught Erica's attention while she and Karen were contacting the dead.

"Did you see that?" she asked. "It was a blue ball of light!"

Joe and I were not surprised that she saw a blue light because one of the ghosts spotted in the graveyard over the years was a black ghost dressed in priestly garb that carried a blue-flamed lantern. Erica knew nothing of this ghost; we didn't tell her about it. She was unaware of the story; so was Karen.

Erica followed the blue light to the western section of the cemetery where four tall monuments rise high above the graves.

Orbs moving through Lakeview Cemetery. *Photo by The Paranormal Adventurers.*

She told us the blue light was moving quickly through the cold night air.

"I still see it!" she said, pointing skyward. "It's right there!"

Though the rest of us could not see the blue orb, we chased it all around the graveyard, snapping pictures wherever Erica pointed.

Our Sony digital camera, which we've dubbed "The Dark Angel" because of its ability to capture paranormal anomalies, caught image after image of the orb flying through the haunted graveyard, sometimes appearing blue, sometimes white.

As I struggled to keep pace with Erica, who was in hot pursuit of the blue orb, the blue anomaly suddenly appeared to me, too.

I yelled to Joe, "It's over there! It's headed toward Waverly Avenue!"

At that instant, I realized I had just uttered the same words I'd read in a newspaper story about the ghost of Lakeview Cemetery.

In the story a young man was chasing the ghost. The reporter said the ghost headed toward Waverly Avenue to escape his

Comet-like orb flying over Sailors' Plot. *Photo by The Paranormal Adventurers.*

pursuer. Now, it was happening again, more than a hundred years later. We were chasing the *spirit* of Lakeview Cemetery through the graves toward Waverly Avenue!

Coincidently, months later, Erica and I shared another experience like this in Oaklawn Cemetery in Brookhaven. After completing an investigation one evening, we were walking on the path around the graveyard when suddenly a bright white ball of light with a comet-like tail flew over us. I was stunned by the anomaly's sudden appearance.

"Did you see that?" Erica asked me.

"What did you see?" I countered, not wanting to reveal what I had seen.

"I saw a light that looked like a comet. It flew right in front of us!" she answered.

"I saw the same thing!" I said excitedly.

With our flashlights we searched the area where we saw the comet-like anomaly. We discovered the sandy gravesite of a recently buried man. His headstone indicated that he had been a fireman. The streaking white orb disappeared right over his grave.

Now on this night at Lakeview Cemetery as we chased the blue orb, the night unexpectedly erupted with paranormal mists as thick as soup that appeared only to Joe's and Karen's cameras.

Karen was drawn to the Sailors' Plot, but it was around the graves of the sailors from the *Nahum Chapin* she felt the strongest energy. She photographed their headstones and, in the light of her camera's flash, Joe could see the ghostly shapes of graveyard spirits now visiting.

In the mid 1800s Spiritualist mediums called such mists "ectoplasm." Mediums often produced ectoplasm during séances, however it was usually faked. They sought to reproduce the white material that appeared to genuine mediums when spirits were truly present.

In our case, the mists appeared in our photographs and, in keeping with the stories reported about the elusive ghosts of Lakeview Cemetery, left the area just as quickly.

Ghostly shapes of visiting graveyard spirits. *Photo by The Paranormal Adventurers.*

Long ago Joe and I had determined that paranormal mists are composed of moisture, not ectoplasm. We determined the temperature in any given place must be low enough for the vapors to be manipulated by the spirits. These mists are not the result of expelled breath or rising vapors from waterholes or streams. Rather, they are accumulated vapors purposely manipulated by spirits to manifest before our eyes. Even spirits must conform to the laws of nature. They cannot create substance out of airy nothing. In this case, moisture is their medium. This is our theory.

In one of the photographs taken that night, the unmistakable face of a spirit stares sadly back at us. The eye is clearly distinguishable as is the nose and mouth, but it is not a human face...it is a *ghostly* face.

What does this spirit want to communicate to us?

In another photograph, we caught what appears to be a face looming in a mist high above us. Is the spirit watching us,

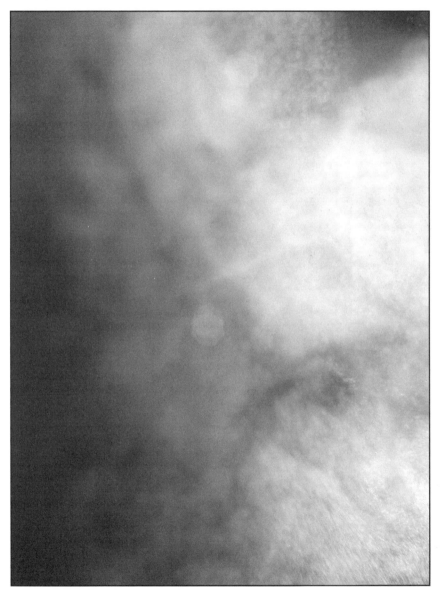

Look closely. Do you see a face forming in this mist?
Photo by The Paranormal Adventurers.

Ghostly face peering down at Lakeview Cemetery.
Photo by The Paranormal Adventurers.

observing our every move, waiting for an opportunity to manifest in its next form as a full-bodied apparition?

Are these the same ghosts that have been reported at Lakeview Cemetery through the centuries?

We believe the answer to these questions is a resounding yes!

View Photographs Online

There are two photographs in particular we would like to show you that have relevance to the story of Lakeview Cemetery. To view these photographs, please visit our website at www.paranormaladventurers.com and follow the links.

† The first photograph shows Joe and another paranormal investigator walking before the Sailors' Plot. Above the graves are light anomalies that were not visible to our naked eyes when we were in the cemetery. Take note of the boomerang

shapes and how the only solid white one is blocking the investigator's face. The solid appearing anomaly was located between the camera and the investigator. Please note the radiation given off by the anomalies in the close-up. What are these? Why did they appear? A psychic who viewed this photograph told us that the white anomaly over the investigator's face is a sign that her presence is not welcome in the graveyard.

† In the second photograph light rods appear over the Sailors' graves. Notice the different colors of the light rods. While we have photographed this type of anomaly in other locations, we do not understand why they appear to our camera or what they mean. A psychic in one of our library audiences told us the rods are an invitation by the spirits to visit the graveyard.

Mist creeping across the graveyard. *Photo by The Paranormal Adventurers.*

Z

Machpelah Cemetery

"If God in His infinite wisdom ever sent an angel upon earth in human form it was my mother."

-- Harry Houdini

Prelude

Harry Houdini must speak to the dead.

At the edge of the park, Houdini's wife, Bess, stops to catch her breath. She's been following him since he left their home. She leans against a tree pulling her long, black cape tightly around to ward off the early evening chill.

Ahead of her, Houdini enters the deserted park. It is now twilight. A pale yellow light casts a glow on the bare autumn trees.

Houdini pounds the wide path. His black boots kick the red and yellow leaves into the air. His hands are shoved deep inside the pockets of his long black coat. His hat is pulled down low over his eyes. He is moving swiftly now through the darkening

Harry Houdini. *Courtesy of Karen Isaksen.*

night. Bess watches him leave the park and pick up his pace. Leaves swirl around his ankles as he hurries across the street to the dark graveyard.

Bess is careful to stay hidden in the shadows. Her husband cannot know she's been following him. She watches as he approaches the heavy wrought iron gate at the entrance to the cemetery. The gate is locked. Bess thinks perhaps now he will end this madness and come home.

Screeching ravens fly in mad circles above him. Houdini grabs the cold black bars of the cemetery gate and shakes them angrily. He must get inside! No lock will keep him out! His fiery eyes burn at the chain and padlock. The circling ravens are suddenly silenced. Houdini drops his hands to his sides and strides through the gate.

Bess yanks up her long skirt and dashes across the street with her black cape flying behind her. She knows what she will see before she reaches the cemetery fence. Harry had thrown himself across his mother's grave! The echoes of his sobs tear at Bess' soul. She watches helplessly as her husband claws at the dirt, begging his mother to speak to him through the casket and earth. He is desperate to communicate with her.

Leaning her head against the cold black wrought iron, Bess squeezes her eyes shut. She cannot bear to witness Harry's agony any longer. She knows what she must do. She must find a medium that can contact Harry's mother through séance.

Harry Houdini must *speak* to the dead.

Harry Houdini throwing himself across his mother's grave.
Courtesy of Karen Isaksen.

The Cemetery

View of Machpelah Cemetery from across Cypress Hills Avenue.
Photo by The Paranormal Adventurers.

Location: 8230 Cypress Hills Street, Ridgewood, Queens, New York

Description: An overcrowded Jewish cemetery with headstones that range from simple slabs to ornate monuments. This cemetery is mostly overgrown and neglected.

How to get there: Grand Central Parkway to Exit 13W – Jackie Robinson Parkway – towards Brooklyn. Take the Jackie Robinson Parkway to Exit 3 (Cypress Hills Street). Turn right at the traffic light and Machpelah Cemetery is the first cemetery on the left.

The Weeping Woman

Death is the essence of this story.

I stand facing the statue of a weeping woman.

This is the grave of Harry Houdini who died October 31, 1926. He was and still is the most famous magician who ever lived.

Machpelah Cemetery on Cypress Hills Street, therefore, is one of the most notable cemeteries in the entire world.

As far as we know, Houdini has never come back from the grave. Today, however, we will experience some of the mystery of Houdini at Machpelah Cemetery.

Death will pull rabbits out of a hat just for us. But the rabbits are... *phantoms, apparitions, ghost lights, and a haunted building.*

The statue of the weeping woman represents the sadness and loss felt by people worldwide when the renowned illusionist died suddenly. She's holding a wreath in her right hand, reminding us that the king is dead.

I climb the white granite steps of the stately memorial where a bronze bust of Houdini once stood overlooking his family's graves. The bust it gone. It has been stolen and replaced several times

over the years. The spot just above the mosaic emblem for the Society of American Magicians is now empty.

Sitting on the bench beside the weeping woman, I can almost hear the sounds of the carnival organ at full tilt and sense the clamor of the pressing crowds cheering for the Great Houdini, the master illusionist.

"Show us a trick!" someone might yell. "Raise the dead!" another might shout.

Machpelah Cemetery is a city of the dead where it seems some ghosts have been raised. Gravestones, like city tenements, crowd in on each other. But Houdini's grave is airy and open as would be expected for a king. His *protector* wanders the grounds as a white-faced phantom we catch glimpses of as we pay tribute to the master.

Large white and brown rocks, purple and amber crystals, and small pebbles lie atop Houdini's flat gravestone. These are signs of love and remembrance. Harry Houdini has not been forgotten. His *protector* will not let us forget as he flies across the graveyard

Houdini's gravesite. *Photo by The Paranormal Adventurers.*

Stones placed atop Houdini's grave by visitors. *Photo by The Paranormal Adventurers.*

in the corner of our vision. When we turn, we see nothing there. We try and turn quickly, but the phantom moves ever faster. We are in a race with the supernatural.

The practice of leaving rocks on a gravestone stems from a tradition that began in ancient times. When someone died, a large boulder was placed in front of the cave that served as a tomb. It was believed the boulder would keep the spirit of the dead from coming out and haunting.

The rocks and glittering crystals on Houdini's gravestone did not keep his spirit in the grave. He had the ability to make his presence known to us.

Houdini's gravestone reads: "And Beloved Wife Wilhelmina Beatrice." In his will, Houdini specifically requested that his loving wife, Bess, be buried with him.

However, that request was not fulfilled. Bess, who was Catholic, was not permitted to be buried beside the husband she adored because Machpelah is a Jewish cemetery.

Their religious differences did not keep them apart in life, but separated them in death. Bess was laid to rest in Gate of Heaven Cemetery in Hawthorne, New York, many miles from her beloved Harry.

‡‡‡‡‡‡‡‡‡

Challenging and Defying Death

It was with true American pride that Harry Houdini told people he was born in Appleton, Wisconsin April 6, 1874. And while his family did live in Appleton, Houdini was actually born in Budapest, Hungary.

Houdini entered the world as Erich Weiss on March 24, 1874. He was the fourth son born to Rabbi Mayer Samuel Weiss and his second wife Cecilia.

For some reason known only to her, Houdini's mother, Cecilia Weiss, changed his birth date from March 24 to April 6. In a letter to one of his brothers shortly after the death of their mother, Harry stated he would always celebrate on April 6 because his mother always wrote him on that date. It would remain his adopted birthday for the remainder of his life.

A traveling circus visiting a small town was big news and Appleton residents turned out to be entertained by the clowns and acrobats. But for one spectator, seven-year-old Erich Weiss, the highlight of the circus was the high wire walker. His death-defying stunts high above the audience kept Erich spellbound. He knew one mistake could send the high wire performer hurling to the ground below.

Watching the performer taunt and cheat death exhilarated the young boy. He was inspired by what he witnessed that day. Thus began a lifelong fascination with death-defying acts.

Houdini became famous for challenging death. He was often locked in safes and lowered into freezing rivers from which he had to escape. He was suspended high above many a city, freeing himself from a straight jacket as people on the street far below watched in rapt fascination.

His original invention, the Water Torture Cell, was a death-defying stunt in which he was suspended upside down with his ankles locked into wooden stocks. He was then lowered into the locked water-filled tank. The possibility of Houdini not escaping from the tank in time thrilled audiences.

Houdini was a master escape artist.

A new word, "houdinize," was coined during the height of Houdini's career. The following is the exact definition as taken from the 1920 edition of *Funk & Wagnall's New Dictionary*:

Hou' di-nize, vt. "To release or extricate oneself from (confinement, bonds, or the like), as by wriggling out."

Erich's Promise

Twelve-year-old Erich stood beside the bed and listened carefully to his father's request. As he spoke, Rabbi Weiss reached for the *Holy Book* he kept on the nightstand and held it out to his son.

Looking into his father's sad brown eyes, Erich, a solemn dark-haired boy, reverently placed his strong hand upon the worn book.

"I promise, father," he intoned.

And with those words, young Erich Weiss, who later grew up to be Harry Houdini, vowed to take care of his mother for the rest of her life.

For a father to impose such a heavy burden on his young son may seem ludicrous, but Rabbi Weiss knew instinctively that Erich would not let him down.

Erich was not the eldest son, but he was the most resourceful. The money he earned was given to his mother at the end of each day. The relief and joy on her face pushed him to work even harder.

Erich Weiss was always the quintessential mama's boy, but after his father's death in 1892, he and his mother grew even closer. Cecilia Weiss was Erich's whole world. She

was a sweet, loving soul with work-worn hands and wise gentle eyes. Erich wanted more than anything to make his mother feel secure and happy. He thought she deserved to be treated like a queen.

Cecilia Weiss, Houdini's mother. *Courtesy of Karen Isaksen.*

The budding magician believed he could achieve fame and fortune as an entertainer using his superior athletic abilities and the skills he learned working for a locksmith. His mother was his greatest motivator.

Erich left home when the family fell upon hard times. His inevitable success would soon provide his mother with a comfortable life and fulfill the promise he made to his father.

Eventually, Houdini purchased an elegant twenty-six room mansion in Harlem. Cecilia Weiss lived there along with Harry and Bess until her death. Cecilia was finally living the life that Harry had envisioned for her.

Houdini was at the pinnacle of his career when he died at age fifty-two of a ruptured appendix, leaving behind his broken-hearted wife, Bess, his brothers, and a sister. Harry and Bess had no children.

Houdini's Death

Theories abound about how Houdini died:

† One theory is that a radical faction of the Spiritualist movement poisoned him because of his quest to expose mediums and séances as fake.

† Some believe the injury that caused his death was brought about by a McGill College student who punched Houdini several times in the stomach while he lay prone on a couch in his dressing room.

† Still others believe Houdini was suffering from appendicitis for several days and did not receive medical attention soon enough because he refused to cancel any performances. He did not want to disappoint his audiences.

† As depicted in the 1953 movie "Houdini," starring Tony Curtis and Janet Leigh, Houdini accidentally ran into a prop sword handle backstage, rupturing his appendix and nearly drowning in the Water Torture Cell that he invented. He is dramatically rescued from the glass water tank only to die onstage in the arms of his wife. This version of his death is high drama and pure Hollywood fiction.

The exact truth of what ultimately led to Houdini's death will never been known. What we do know is that on October 31, 1926, the world lost the greatest illusionist whoever lived. There will never be another Houdini.

Thousands of people lined the streets for Houdini's funeral hoping to see if he could pull off the greatest feat of his career. Could he bring himself back from the dead?

‡‡‡‡‡‡‡‡‡‡

Arriving at the Cemetery

Nobody was on Cypress Hills Street the first time we visited Machpelah Cemetery.

Cemeteries line both sides of the street. It's a corridor of the dead.

If Long Island had tumbleweed, it would have been rolling down this road. We *felt* watched. We *sensed* unseen spirits. This has happened to us on Sweet Hollow Road in Melville and on the battlefields of Gettysburg, Pennsylvania. The air is thick with spirit energy...*you can cut it with a knife.*

Machpelah Cemetery is not what we anticipated. We expected trimmed yellow bushes, flowering pink trees, lush green grass, and bubbling marble fountains. Instead, blue graffiti slashes across the façade of a drab beige building that once served as the

Dangerous barbed wire on rusted fence keeps vandals from entering the cemetery at night. *Photo by The Paranormal Adventurers.*

cemetery's office. Now we are greeted by this rundown building with peeling paint and rolls of steely barbed wire atop a rusted chain link fence to keep people out. A black cat with yellow eyes stares at us from one of the broken windows.

We can't stay out: the spirits are *luring* us into the cemetery. The dead *must* speak to us.

A man stares down at us from a window on the second floor as we drive through the gate. Joe and I wonder who he is and if he's going to give us a hard time about being on the property. His long sleeved white shirt appeared clean and pressed, in the style of Houdini. He doesn't move the whole time we are in the cemetery.

Is he human or is he an apparition? We believe he is an apparition. Visit our website to review the video we shot of him and see if you agree.

Joe and I couldn't shake the feeling that eyes were following us the entire time we were there that day. Though we concentrated

Look at the window on the second floor. A man stares down at us without moving. Is he real or an apparition? *Photo by The Paranormal Adventurers.*

Abandoned cemetery office building with the staircase going to the basement. Initially the basement door was partially open. When we checked it two hours later, it was closed but nobody had been there except for us. *Photo by The Paranormal Adventurers.*

on tasks at hand, part of our thoughts were stuck to that building, which we glanced at often.

At one point, we crept close to a staircase leading down to an open basement door of the abandoned building. As Joe carefully made his way down the steps, amid broken glass, I couldn't help but feel it will turn out badly if he opens the door all the way and enters the mysteriously haunted basement. My concern is not that homeless people might be living there, but the spirits that dwell within may not want uninvited visitors. The air is palatable with spirit presence.

We go back to our work, photographing Houdini's gravesite. After we've finished, we revisit the open door in the basement, but find that it is now firmly shut. There are no people around. We never heard the door shut. By the end of the day we conclude it must have been the protector who we caught fleeting glimpses of throughout our visit.

Machpelah Cemetery is a ghost of what it once was. The grandeur of the old graveyard is lost among weeds. Many of the graves are neglected and overgrown. Wild ivy snakes its way around forgotten gravestones and tall wheat-colored weeds all but obliterate the ornate and intricately carved brown and gray monuments.

In the midst of this chaos, Houdini's manicured and neat gravesite stands out like a bright oasis.

A committee of volunteers from the New York Chapter of the Society of American Magicians maintains the gravesite by cutting the grass and removing assorted items left behind by fans. We once found a witch's broomstick lying across Houdini's grave.

The protector, meanwhile, keeps silent watch over the master.

Communicating with the Spirits

We are the only visitors in the graveyard on this late spring afternoon. The sun creates long shadows over the many graves.

I step carefully over the rusted nails and broken glass scattered in the tiny parking area as I make my way toward the path that will take me to Houdini's family plot.

The family gravestones are spread out before me. His beloved mother, father, brothers, sister, and grandmother are all buried here.

The sudden chill creeping up my spine alerts me to the fact that I'm not alone. There is a spirit energy surrounding me—I'm awed by its powerful presence. It's a positive energy. I feel as though it wants to communicate with me.

I walk toward the grave of Houdini's mother, Cecilia Weiss. Kneeling down, I place my hand gingerly on the stone. It's warm from the afternoon sunlight. My hand is tingling. A feeling of calm radiates throughout my body.

I begin to speak in hushed tones. I thank her for bringing such a warm and talented man into the world. I thank her for being

such a positive force in her son's life. I thank her for encouraging him and believing in him. I tell her he became the great man he was because of her.

I find a shiny black stone hidden in the grass. I pick it up and press it to my lips before placing it on her gravestone.

Slowly, I rise to my feet. A warm breeze caresses my face. It feels like the loving hand of a mother. I think perhaps Cecilia is acknowledging me. I smile.

I walk over and stand before the grave of the greatest magician who ever lived. I look down and see Bess' name engraved on the gravestone. There is only a date of birth, no date of death.

A feeling of sadness washes over me. Harry lies alone in his grave. It was his wish that Bess be buried beside him, but that wish was not granted.

I take solace in the fact his beloved mother is near. His head rests upon packets of letters she wrote to him while he was away on tours.

I drop to my knees. Amber and purple crystals, small stones, rocks, and blue and white playing cards adorn Houdini's gravestone. More than eighty years after his death there are still many fans that remember and honor him. I am touched by their devotion.

"Harry," I whisper, "people still love and admire you. You left your mark on our world. So many magicians imitate you. Maybe you wouldn't be pleased about that, but they say imitation is the sincerest form of flattery. It's their way of honoring you."

I pick up the largest rock I can find and place it on the corner of his gravestone.

"I *feel* your energy, Harry. Could you please show me a sign of your presence?"

I lay my hand gently on the gravestone, careful not to disturb any of the stones or crystals. Closing my eyes, I whisper a silent prayer, asking Houdini if he would honor me by communicating with me in some way.

I get to my feet and walk to the white granite steps. Climbing up, I sit beside the statue of the weeping woman. I reach out and stroke her head. A feeling of peace envelops me.

I take my pendulum from my pocket and hold it between my hands. With my eyes closed, I take several long deep breaths.

Tree branches begin to sway wildly and their green leaves do a primal dance, as the wind suddenly grows stronger. I'm not sure I can use my pendulum in these conditions, but the spirit energy is so powerful, I must try.

I hold the slim silver chain of the pendulum between my thumb and forefinger of my left hand. The translucent pointed crystal at the opposite end of the chain is moving in the same direction the wind is blowing.

I murmur a prayer to the universe asking for help in communicating with the spirit of Harry Houdini.

With the pendulum swaying in the wind, I hold it in front of me and ask as I normally do, "Show me 'yes' please."

To my surprise, the pendulum begins to move back and forth, the sign it always shows me for "yes."

Thinking the wind probably shifted, I ask the pendulum, "Show me 'no' please." I am amazed as the pendulum switches directions and moves from side to side, the sign it always shows me for "no."

Still skeptical, I ask, "Show me 'maybe' please." In the blowing wind, the pendulum shifts directions again and is now moving in a circular motion, the sign it always shows me for "maybe."

I am grateful the spirits and the universe are working with me.

I am alone. Joe has gone outside the cemetery gates to take photographs from across the street.

Holding the pendulum in front of me, I ask the first question.

"Harry, is there a heaven?" The pendulum sways back and forth, answering yes.

"Harry, do you know you are the most famous magician in the world?" The pendulum again sways back and forth, but

with a little more force, letting me know he is quite aware of his iconic status.

"Harry, if you had it to do over, would you have gone to the hospital sooner?" The pendulum continues to swing back and forth, but slower, almost regretfully, this time.

"Harry, did you want to die?" The pendulum immediately switches directions to indicate a definite "NO."

But the most emphatic answer comes when I ask, "Harry, is your mother with you?" The "yes" I receive is so forceful it nearly causes me to drop the pendulum!

Joe comes back into the cemetery's parking area. I can't wait to tell him what happened to me, but the look on his face stops me cold.

"Someone has been watching me," he says.

"Who?" I ask. "There is no one else here."

"A phantom," Joe replies. "I can feel its eyes following me everywhere I go. It's trying to scare us away. I think it's *the protector* we've been seeing all afternoon."

Joe and I are only a few feet apart. The energy I'm feeling is strong and welcoming...so unlike what Joe is feeling. How can the energy be so different and why?

Joe begins to pan the rundown building and surrounding graves with the video camera. With a frightened screech, a black bird suddenly shoots out from a dark cluster trees looming over the graveyard.

A second later, Joe catches a white-faced phantom lurking in black shadows. It's the same phantom we have been glimpsing all afternoon.

In the video, the ghostly white face of the phantom can be seen bobbing and weaving back and forth like a punch-drunk boxer. On video we can see his shoe sticking out of the shadows.

When Joe puts the camera down and observes the area with his naked eyes to see why the bird was so scared, he sees only darkness amid the trees. The phantom has vanished as quickly

as it appeared. He didn't want us to get to know him. He just wanted us to know he was there.

Joe walks over to me feeling uneasy.

"Did you see him?" he asks. "He was hiding among those trees over there." He points to the dark shadows.

"I didn't see anything but the bird," I answer.

Joe studies the trees. He is lost in his own thoughts. His mind's eye plays out the scene he viewed through the lens of the video camera. An apparition had shown itself to him. He caught it on video.

Later that day, when we returned to our studio, Joe watches the video over and over again. Each time it's as if it's the first. And each time, he gropes for answers.

"But maybe it wasn't a bad thing," I say as I look over at the trees where he saw the phantom. "Maybe he truly *is* the graveyard's *protector*. If he thought you were here to disrespect Harry Houdini or the graveyard, he probably would have done something more."

Joe thought about it for a moment. He didn't answer. His eyes told the story. The essence of the story is death. He takes one last uneasy look over his shoulder.

‡‡‡‡‡‡‡‡‡

Broken Wand Ceremony

For many years on October 31 at 1:26 p.m., the time of Houdini's departure from this life, the Broken Wand Ceremony was held at Machpelah Cemetery. However, because the crowds became too big, and in some cases, unruly, the date was changed. It's now held on the anniversary of Houdini's death according to the Jewish calendar. The actual date changes every year, but it always falls within the month of November.

I stand in front of Houdini's gravestone. Joe points the video camera at me as I explain the origin of the Broken Wand Ceremony.

"The Broken Wand Ceremony was created to honor the life of Harry Houdini," I begin. "It symbolized the joy and pleasure the master illusionist brought to audiences, but now can no longer be because he passed into another realm."

Just as I utter the words "passed into another realm," a white object passes in front of my face. Neither Joe nor I saw it when it happened. It was only visible to us once we watched the video back in our studio.

We studied the video clip over and over. We slowed it down and made it a still photograph. We showed it to other investigators and everyone agreed it was not a bug, butterfly, moth, or feather. The consensus was it was **NOT** *of this world*. It was a supernatural occurrence that paranormal investigators commonly refer to as a *ghost light*.

Each time I watch the video, I feel so privileged. Between the pendulum, the ghost light, and even the phantom, I know there were spirits among us. I felt the gentle spirit of Houdini's mother and the strong presence of her beloved son.

I feel as though I have a special connection with Harry Houdini. This was validated during a presentation we did at Suffolk Community College in Selden.

As part of the program, we showed the video of the phantom of Machpelah Cemetery. Afterward, a young lady who possesses psychic abilities told me as I spoke about Houdini she saw a bright orb hovering around above my head. That made sense to me because I feel very connected to him.

She smiled and said, "He likes you!"

Where Are You, Harry?

Houdini never came through during the yearly Halloween séances Bess held. It has been said the veil between the realms is the thinnest on Halloween so contacting the other side during this time should be easier. So why didn't he ever make contact through a séance? Are séances and mediums fake as Houdini proved to the world over and over before he died? Is death truly the end?

If Houdini was such an adamant non-believer in séances, why then did he bother to write a secret message and leave it with Bess? He instructed her that if this message was ever conveyed during a séance she would know for sure Houdini was coming through from the other side. Clearly, he wanted to believe there was an afterlife.

The one thing Houdini wanted most in the world was to communicate with his mother after she passed away. He was totally devoted to her in life and obsessed with contacting her after her death.

Death Haunts Houdini

Houdini stood on deck of a steamer blowing kisses to his mother as she waved to him from the pier. He was off to Europe where he was scheduled to perform for the King of Sweden. The date was July 8, 1913. It was the last time Houdini would ever see his mother alive.

Cecilia Weiss, age 72, died July 17, 1913 after suffering a massive stroke.

Houdini collapsed when he read the cable informing him of his mother's death.

Guilt haunted him for the rest of his life.

"I should have been there, sitting by her bedside, comforting her, holding her hand, and kissing her good-bye." Houdini thought.

She was the love of his life and now she had moved beyond his reach.

Harry never forgave himself for not being with her when she took her last breath. But more than that, he needed to know his mother forgave him for not being there when she needed him the most.

His mother's body was laid out in a coffin that was placed in the parlor of their home. After seeing her lying in repose, Harry wrote this in his diary: "She looked so dainty and restful, only a small spot on Her cheek and The Face which haunted me with love all my Life is still and quiet, and when She does not answer me I know God is taking Her to His bosom and giving Her the peace which she denied herself on this earth."

In his desperation to contact her, he turned to séances and mediums at a time when the Spiritualist movement was experiencing a resurgence in the United States because of the lives lost during World War I.

Harry often disguised himself and visited dozens of mediums and participated in séances. He was outraged when he discovered phony sleight-of-hand tricksters and false prophets who called themselves Spiritualists were duping him. Thus began a war that raged between Houdini and the Spiritualists movement that lasted until his untimely death in 1926.

Reunited at Long Last

I have thought long and hard about why Houdini failed to come through during Bess' séances and subsequent séances held after her death. If anyone is strong enough to speak from the other side, it is definitely Houdini. It is my theory that the unbridled happiness he felt at being reunited with his mother in death overshadowed his need to come back and communicate with anyone, even Bess.

Perhaps Houdini was finally able to reunite with his mother on October 31, 1926 at 1:26 p.m. ... the moment he passed from this life to the next. Maybe she was there to greet him. He had waited thirteen long years for this moment. One can only imagine the joyous reunion; mother and son together once again, this time for eternity.

As long as he was with his mother, he could patiently wait for the day Bess would finally join them. At long last, Harry Houdini may well have found the peace and contentment that eluded him during his hectic lifetime.

‡‡‡‡‡‡‡‡‡

The wind has died down. The trees are swaying gently, almost as if they are bidding us goodbye. When we reach the car, I turn to take one last look at Houdini's gravesite. I feel as though I'm leaving an old friend.

Spirits surrounded Joe and me that afternoon. Ghost hunters should not miss this haunting experience.

When you visit Machpelah Cemetery, take a moment and sit beside the statue of the weeping woman. Quiet your mind and open your heart. You may feel the gentle caress of Cecilia Weiss, the dynamic energy of Harry Houdini, or the watchful eyes of the elusive phantom *protector*.

We are grateful to have had the opportunity to feel their presence.

Harry Houdini was a man who was bigger than life and even bigger in death. The king may be dead, but his legacy and his spirit live on at Machpelah Cemetery.

"The magic of earth is over. The magic and mystery of another realm awaits him and will be revealed. May God bless the life of Harry Houdini."

-- from the Broken Wand Ceremony

3

Pine Hollow Cemetery

Entrance to haunted Pine Hollow Cemetery. *Photo by The Paranormal Adventurers.*

 Chapter Three: Pine Hollow Cemetery

Location: Off Route 106 in Oyster Bay

Description: Pine Hollow is a small historic cemetery, only several acres big with perhaps two hundred graves.

How to get there: This cemetery is located on a small street, just south of the Mill-Max building off the west side of Pine Hollow Road (the local name for Route 106) in Oyster Bay. Route 106 can be reached by the Long Island Expressway at Exit 41 North. From the LIE go north and stay to the right as Route 106 and Route 107 fork away from each other with 106 quickly veering to the right. The cemetery is located across the street from a strip mall in which a CVS and a Dunkin Donuts are located.

‡‡‡‡‡‡‡‡‡‡

Ghost on the Hill

The ghost appeared in clothing the color of a funeral hearse — stark black.

He wore a flaring black cape and a strange round hat that shadowed his gray face. There was no humor about him. He was a ghost back from the grave. The grim vision was as cold as a kiss to a dead person's lips at a wake.

"He was just standing there looking at me," recalled Erica Popino. The 43-year-old Holtsville resident visibly shuddered as she told her story of the dead man's ghost appearing to her.

All around her sat members of a large audience at Sachem Public Library in Holbrook where she appeared as *The Paranormal Adventurers*' guest speaker that night.

Children sat huddled together on the floor at the front of the auditorium, hypnotized by the low lighting and spooky stories of spirits escaping the grave. Dozens of adults stood around the perimeter of the room because there were not enough seats to accommodate all the people—most showed up to see evidence of spirit activity on Long Island.

All eyes were upon our guest. The hushed faces gazed up at her, transfixed on her every word.

"It was daytime," Popino started, speaking slowly. "I was alone up on the hill at Pine Hollow Cemetery in Oyster Bay. I heard a hawk scream in the sky, so I looked up at it. When I looked back down, there was a man standing twenty feet away from me, just staring at me. He appeared out of nowhere."

Popino, a seasoned ghost investigator, began seeing ghosts and spirit manifestations after she had a near death experience as a child.

She has photographed spirits expressing themselves in the forms of orbs, hazes, and mists. She seeks out ghost hunting adventures in Long Island graveyards and haunted houses to advance her knowledge of the *other side*. On voice recorders she has captured spirits speaking in "white noise."

Popino told the audience she had visited Pine Hollow Cemetery on a whim the morning she saw the ghost of the man dressed in all black.

"I was in the area. I saw the cemetery from the road, so I decided to stop in," she explained.

What happened next would begin a macabre dance between Popino and the ghost of Pine Hollow Cemetery that may still be in progress. It might only conclude when investigators uncover who the spirit is and why he haunts that cemetery.

Upon seeing the man standing in front of her, staring at her, Popino continued, "I screamed, 'Jesus Christ!' With that, the man just...vanished!"

"Then what?" asked a boy in the audience.

"I did what any good ghost hunter would do," said Popino, "I ran to my car and cried."

Some people in the audience laughed at the image of a ghost investigator running to her car and crying because she saw a ghost.

Crying is a common release for the tempest of tension and unfamiliar feelings people experience when they see ghosts. Over the years stories have been told about people whose hair turned white, never spoke again, and went blind or stark raving mad upon seeing a ghost.

When I was fifteen, some of my friends began crying when we saw a ghost at a creek in Oceanside. The haunting lasted an hour. The event overloaded our nerve circuits and jangled our emotions. The unnatural sighting of a supernatural being was simply overwhelming for all of us.

Seeing that ghost is a burden I will carry for the rest of my life.

Knowledge of beings from another dimension is knowledge that perhaps we should not possess.

But, like Popino, if we explore the mystery of the *other side* and find answers that may one day help people by bringing them comfort or possibly hope of being reunited with loved ones who have died, then the burden will ultimately become a blessing.

Ghosts themselves are usually not as frightening as their sudden, unexpected appearance. Their pale demeanors often fill witnesses with a morbid dread they will never lose. A ghost's face, then, becomes a dark symbol of Death that inevitably lurks up the road awaiting our arrival.

A lady from the front row in the library audience called out, "I would cry, too, if I saw *THAT* ghost! Dressed in all black...that would scare the hell out of me!"

Audience members nodded in agreement.

‡‡‡‡‡‡‡‡‡‡

A Haunted History

Pine Hollow Cemetery is an extraordinarily haunted graveyard. Ghost hunters investigating this cemetery have experienced

Some people see a skull and some people see a man walking with a stick inside the mist. What do you see? *Photo by The Paranormal Adventurers.*

apparitions, paranormal mists, and barrages of orbs, ghostly growls in the night, and a host of other supernatural activity. This graveyard warrants intense study from ghost investigators who can give it their time.

In one photograph taken at the cemetery, which Diane and I have seen, an area of earth the size of a manhole cover appears to be spinning around like a whirlpool. Out of this vortex a slender white figure rises. Reportedly, a psychic told the man who took the photograph that the white figure was the ghost of a black woman who was a dancer before she died and was buried in Pine Hollow. The psychic said every September the ghost of the dancer rises from her grave to dance.

Pine Hollow Cemetery was virtually unknown to the Long Island paranormal community before Popino had her encounter with the ghost on the hill.

Her story quickly flew from one person to another across the Internet. The news of the ghost's appearance in Oyster Bay instantly fired up interest in the cemetery. Within days, an investigation was planned, continuing the dance between Popino and the spirit wandering the hill there. Only now, dozens more ghost investigators would walk out onto the dirt floor of the Pine Hollow graveyard to have a dance with Death and its mysterious apparitions.

This small, abundantly green burial ground is located in the gentle rolling hills of old Oyster Bay. Back in the late 1800s and early 1900s it was known as a "negro" or "colored" cemetery because African-Americans from the area were historically the only people buried in its soil.

Seven black men who fought in the Civil War are buried in plots in Pine Hollow. One of the men, David Carll, lived locally and raised a family at their nearby home. His grave and the graves of his wife, children, and grandchildren populate the same haunted hill upon which Popino saw the man dressed in all black.

Pine Hollow is not a well-appointed graveyard. Though it is still an "active" cemetery, with bodies of deceased persons continuing to be buried there, no paved roads lead into or out of the grounds.

View of the cemetery's haunted hill from the entrance.
Photo by The Paranormal Adventurers.

Instead, a grassy path leads into the cemetery and cuts left, going southward along an old chain-link fence. On the right side of the fence is the graveyard, extending way back into towering trees that climb up a hill. On the other side of the fence, tucked between Route 106 and the cemetery, is a patch of scraggly woods from which investigators claimed to have heard an unearthly growl one night. In fact, they heard the ghostly growl during the first investigation following Popino's experience with the ghost in the black cape and round hat.

Occasionally, while investigating, Diane and I have noticed freshly dug graves and funeral flowers around new plots. Because of the earth's high sand content in this location, the turned earth of the fresh plots is orange in color, like the color of alley cats.

Striking reds, yellows, and purples of funeral flowers and their black plastic vases stand in sharp contrast to the orange sand.

All around the graveyard stand tall trees with dark trunks and far-reaching boughs. The trees' green tops sway in the cool

winds blowing off the blue waters of Oyster Bay only a mile or so to the north.

In summer, the grass of the cemetery is deep green and large leaves fill the flourishing maple trees. If you are quiet, when the wind blows at night, you can hear the breezes talking among the rustling leaves. In the black velvet sky a million stars twinkle. Don't look up too long lest you look down to see a man in all black standing in front of you.

The biggest trees in the graveyard are old pines with hundreds of broken branch stubs sticking out of their sides like rungs of Jack's beanstalk ladder. The broken branches give testimony to the apocalyptic storms the cemetery encountered on nights when lightening surely must have struck the graves. If they could talk, what tales of ghosts might the trees tell?

One tree in particular is a never-ending source of strange paranormal mists. It's the tallest and thickest granddaddy pine of them all and it towers knowingly over the silent dead buried

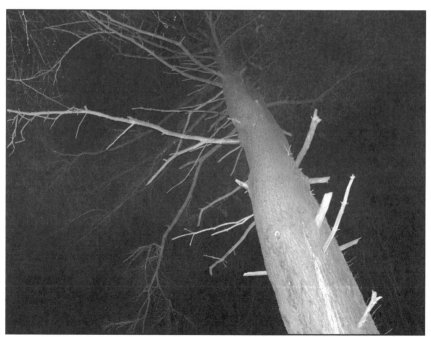

The haunted tree. *Photo by The Paranormal Adventurers.*

below. One can literarlly photograph mists moving around and up and down the tree. The mists can be seen in the light of the camera's flash and can be viewed in photographs—but they *cannot* be detected with naked eyes.

No one has yet figured out the esoteric meaning of these mysterious mists, other than to conclude they might be cryptic manifestations of ghosts. The ghosts, then, are hovering above us and are watching us.

Perhaps the Carll children used to climb this tree. Maybe at one time there was even a tree house in it. Perhaps the spirits of the graveyard congregate around the tree. Whatever the reason, we've detected paranormal activity in and around the tree. *(Some of the mist manifestations can be seen online at our website. Then you should plan a visit to the cemetery and try to photograph them yourself.)*

The parking lot outside the entrance to the cemetery is an overgrown, bumpy, dirt parking field where large chunks of broken concrete were dumped in tall weeds. The debris was probably discarded by contractors looking to save a few bucks on waste management costs. No doubt, the polluters decided to unload their construction debris at the site because few people would notice.

I wonder if the ghost in black visits these contactors – or whoever is responsible for the debris – at night in their dreams now. Be careful how you treat the property of the dead so your sins don't come back to haunt you.

The parking lot is only large enough to accommodate about five cars, and only if they are parked side-by-side. Otherwise only three cars will fit.

One can envision a glossy black hearse on a pale winter morning backing up to the frozen graveyard in a cloud of dissipating exhaust in the biting winter air. The hearse backs up through the small garbage-strewn lot to the space under the cemetery's white archway.

Once backed in straight, the hearse might then be backed up farther into the graveyard to properly unload a shiny brown oak casket for burial. Certainly, the task of a funeral must be arduous

in this graveyard, for most of the property is on an incline or decline. The casket would have to be removed from the hearse and carried by hand through the watery sunlight while crows in the pine trees above scream in complaint at the pallbearers.

Wheels will not roll on this rough terrain. One can only hope the men don't trip and spill the corpse out of the casket. The shivering gravediggers waiting off to the side with sweatshirt hoodies on their heads have to fill the six foot deep hole with the alley cat-orange sand they had gutted from the earth just a day or two before. The gravediggers would be in a hurry to get out of there and leave the haunted place to its own devices.

The tall weeds and scraggly trees facing the busy road outside the cemetery block the view of drivers zooming indifferently along Route 106. The north–south state road is known locally as Pine Hollow Road.

A chain-link fence gate at the entrance to the cemetery is dilapidated and rusty. Sections are broken and hang down towards

View of Route 106 from inside Pine Hollow. *Photo by The Paranormal Adventurers.*

the ground. The white sign arching over the entrance to the graveyard announces "Pine Hollow Cemetery, Founded 1884" on a flimsy sheet of thin wood nailed onto wooden poles. The sign promises to fall victim to a hurricane some day.

From inside the cemetery at night one sees cars passing on Route 106. One can also see people getting in and out of their cars in the parking lot across the street in the strip mall and hear them talking on their cell phones as they walk in and our of stores. It's like a one-way mirror. At night the cemetery is invisible to the rest of the world, but the rest of the world is not invisible to the cemetery.

‡‡‡‡‡‡‡‡‡‡

Hide and Seek

One cold night, months after Popino's experience with the ghost on the hill and after we subsequently investigated the graveyard with a few different paranormal groups, Diane and I, along with Popino and ghost investigator Mike Saliva from Old Bethpage, were on the hill in the dark of the graveyard when three Nassau County Police cars pulled into the tiny parking lot in front of the cemetery. They lined up one next to the other at the entrance at the very spot where hearses must back up under the archway to unload their dead. After the cop cars pulled into the lot, they sat idling. We thought we were being watched by the police officers, but we soon realized the officers could not see us.

At first we thought the cops had arrived at the cemetery to chase us out. After all, they had quickly pulled into the parking lot as if they were on urgent business. When we realized they were not there for us, but for a dinner break or a meeting, we covered up the reflective items we had exposed to the moon and lowered ourselves to the ground and lay flat against the hillside so as not to be spotted. We were afraid we'd be seen if we didn't act quickly.

The ground grew colder as the minutes ticked by. We discussed in whispers the option of grabbing our photography equipment, including tripods, camera cases, and backpacks full of other gear, and going down the hill to exit the cemetery even though the police cars were blocking our only exit. We would certainly be spotted right away as we walked by the police cars.

After a short discussion, we decided that if we tried to leave the graveyard now we would likely scare the police officers to death. We would frighten them by appearing suddenly in front of their windshields. In the dark they might think our equipment was military gear or guns. Even worse, they might think *WE* were spirits moving in the night!

We concluded we'd rather wait till they left before trying to make an exit from the cemetery.

We were not breaking the law by being in Pine Hollow nor were we causing harm to the cemetery. But we lay low and still against the hillside just the same so as not to be detected by the officers.

After a half-hour, the police cars were still there. We decided to inch our way up the side of the haunted hill and into a crevice running up to the higher peaks of hills. This is an area far back behind the cemetery. At least halfway up we could hide behind a stand of trees and huddle together to keep warm till the cops left.

Our bodies were now nearly frozen from hugging the cold damp ground. We looked up into the dark swarm of trees blotting the sky on the hilly horizon high above us, thinking we might find a path cutting into woods at the top of one of those hills. Maybe we could find a street to walk along so we could get back to our cars at the strip mall across Route 106.

The four of us crawled up the hill, through the thick layers of leaves, putting ourselves in jeopardy of falling into a hole or into a hidden roll of discarded barbed wire.

Suddenly, lights of one of the police cars fired on, then another set of headlights flared into the night, and finally the last car's headlights beamed into the darkness. The police cars shot out of the dirt lot with the same urgency with which they had arrived.

We watched them vanish on the other side of the bare winter trees onto Route 106 and into the mad night.

Most of the walking in the cemetery is up and down inclines. The hill begins its climb upwards upon walking into the graveyard.

Houses exist high up behind the cemetery. These houses have lights on at night, but the lights do not interfere with the ghost photography unless the cameras are aimed directly up the hills. Dogs sometimes bark from the backyards of these houses. We have never seen a loose dog in the graveyard, but it's something of which ghost hunters should be aware.

Bordering the north side of the cemetery and shadowing some of the graves, is the tall white cinder block wall of the Mill-Max plant. The building abuts the cemetery's fence. Mill-Max is a manufacturer of precision machined interconnecting components used in industry.

At night a light aimed into the plant's front lot also shines into the front of the cemetery. The light casts a hollow glow over some of the graves at the front of the cemetery near a tool shed where gravediggers store their shovels for the morbid job of digging graves in the alley cat sand.

There is no gate to keep people out of Pine Hollow Cemetery. There's not even a sign saying the graveyard closes at dusk.

The cemetery just exists, always open, it seems, always there...but, seemingly, forgotten by everyone except the people who have loved ones buried there.

‡‡‡‡‡‡‡‡‡

A Hollywood Connection

The cemetery is located near the former Carll family compound, which was located in the hills behind the cemetery. This is where the Carll family lived for generations. It's likely the Carll children, who later simplified their names to "Carl," played in the cemetery,

climbing trees and playing hide-and-seek. Perhaps they even hunted deer and wild turkey on the grounds. The family patriarch was David Carll, who survived being shot through the left lung during a battle in the Civil War.

According to a *Newsday* article about David Carll and his descendents, Carll purchased the land for the compound with the $300 he earned as a soldier. He also bought a schooner that he sailed out of Oyster Bay. He hauled freight along the Atlantic Coast. He died in 1910 and was buried in Pine Hollow Cemetery.

A small American flag is changed often at his gravesite so that the reds, whites, and blues are always clean and bold.

A brass Civil War emblem stands on a small pole beside his grave. David Carll was a soldier in Company 1 of the United States 26th Colored Infantry. The letters CLD. INF. etched into his gravestone stand for "Colored Infantry."

David Carll was an outstanding soldier in the Civil War, but he was much more than a soldier who fought to free slaves. He was a forward thinking man married to a white woman at a time when prejudice against blacks was fierce in Oyster Bay.

Carll did not have an easy life because of the color of his skin. His wife was the daughter of an English yeoman. They were married shortly before he enlisted in the Union Army.

According to records, Carll was one of thirty-seven black men out of approximately five hundred men from Oyster Bay who enlisted in the army to fight in the Civil War.

Members of the Carll family maintained their low-profile lives at the compound that

Grave of Civil War soldier David Carll.
Photo by The Paranormal Adventurers.

The haunted hill. *Photo by The Paranormal Adventurers.*

David Carll founded. They farmed and took care of their livestock. They strived to be self-sufficient because David Carll and his wife did not want to subject their children to the screaming prejudice that faced them in town. They preferred to be isolated from the ugly behavior of white people who mistreated them on the streets.

As they died off over the years, many of David Carll's descendants were also buried in Pine Hollow Cemetery.

David Carll's grave rests in a prominent spot on the incline of a hill that is located in line with the cemetery's entrance. Around him are the interred bodies of his wife, their children, and grandchildren. Also on this hill are members of the Williams family. One of the Carl daughters married a member of the Williams family. A descendant of the Williams and Carl families is Vanessa Williams, the first black Miss America, now a popular and well-known actress.

‡‡‡‡‡‡‡‡‡

The Orb on the Hill

The night of the second investigation at Pine Hollow Cemetery had finally arrived. It promised to be a grand affair.

Diane and I could not attend the first investigation that had been held a few weeks earlier because of our busy speaking engagement schedule, but we heard from those who had participated that it yielded interesting results for some of the ghost investigators who attended.

We were NOT going to miss this hunt. We wanted to see if the ghost would interact with Popino again or, perhaps, with all of us.

Many weeks had now passed since Erica had seen the man appear and disappear on the cemetery hill. In that time fall had turned to winter and the days had grown darker and shorter. A cold wind now blew steadily off the gentle waves of the bay nearby and one could taste the salt whipped in the air. The blue waters of the Long Island Sound had changed to steel gray with the reflection of the brooding winter clouds passing in the forlorn sky like the Canadian geese that had mostly departed for islands south by now.

The flourishing maple trees of Pine Hollow Cemetery, with their dark supple leaves, were now bare. The leaves had dried up, turned brown, and fallen into a new layer on the ground that would eventually rot into the soil. The deep green summer grass of the cemetery has now turned sere and no longer grows. Squawking black crows fly from one tree to another in cawing complaint of visitors to their private graveyard.

You could almost imagine the black birds screaming in their guttural caws:

"Get out!"
"This is no place for you!"
"Get out! Get out while you still can!"

Nearly twenty members of P.A.S.T. would descend upon this haunted cemetery this winter's evening. P.A.S.T. is the acronym for Paranormal Activity Study Team. It's a Yahoo.com group for which there is no membership fee or dues. Anyone is welcome to join. *(You can visit P.A.S.T. at http://tech.groups.yahoo.com/ group/Paranormal_Activity_Study_Team/).*

On this night, ghost hunters and friends would join together to do what we love to do best: try to reach the spirits. Tonight we would move about in the cover of darkness with the goal of gaining insight into the ghosts that dwell within Pine Hollow Cemetery.

There are a handful of basic questions most of us want to answer:

† **How do ghosts happen?**

† **What is the mechanism by which they come back?**

† **How do they materialize?**

We met at the Dunkin Donuts in the strip mall on Route 106, across from the bleak graveyard. Diane and I were late, but the group kindly waited for us.

Members of our large team surely must have looked like North Pole explorers to drivers who spotted us in their headlights as we attempted to cross the dangerously dark road to get to the cemetery. Some of us carried a lot of equipment; I carried a tripod and two camera cases and a daypack on my back.

Once in the cemetery, I would set up our video camera on the tripod and then carry around one of our still cameras — the one we lovingly call the "Dark Angel" because of its unparalleled ability to catch paranormal phenomena. We would each keep a keen eye out for unusual activity and photograph anything we thought was out of the ordinary.

Some members of the group were using voice recorders to try and capture **Electronic Voice Phenomenon** (EVP).

Still others with psychic talents would use their extraordinary sensitivity to *feel*, *hear*, and *see* the spirits.

Some ghost hunters use **EMF detectors** that register electrical spikes or infrared thermometers that gauge temperature changes. Jumping electrical fields might indicate elevated electricity in the air. A sudden drop in temperature indicates cold spots. These tools are used to let us know when we are in an area of physical change, which could be indication that there is spirit energy around.

On this night in Pine Hollow Cemetery we wanted to make contact with the ghostly man Popino had seen on the hill, the apparition she described as looking like "Zorro." Most of us wanted to witness his dead face the same way Popino had seen it.

Seeing the ghost in the black cape would come at a steep price, of course. It would be an experience none of us would ever forget. In addition, there is always the risk that the spirit might follow us and haunt us at home.

Two ladies who joined the group this night brought their children along. They had been on investigations with us before and the children were always respectful and well-behaved, and have a keen interest in ghosts.

Suddenly, one of the children, a ten-year-old boy, screamed. Members of the group rushed to him. He was trembling and crying. He said he was *punched* in the side by a something he could not see. Tears streamed down his red cheeks and his breathing was in short gasps.

His mother lifted his shirt to examine the area. There was a bright red mark that appeared over his abdomen. He was terribly frightened. We tried to comfort and reassure him.

The incident occurred in an area where some investigators had experienced activity in this cemetery. That evening investigators had reported seeing shadows and had the feeling they were being watched. Orbs and other strange light anomalies appeared to our cameras. Everyone on the hunt was upset over the boy getting punched and we were all on high alert.

Subsequently, the woman with the children dropped out of the group. We can only hope the punch that the boy received from the spirit does not scar him psychologically. This is exactly the kind of episode that baffles ghost investigators.

Naturally, we all wanted to photograph the phenomenon of a ghost appearance while were at Pine Hollow Cemetery. If at all possible, we also wanted to communicate directly with the spirit – *or spirits* – that dwell there to ascertain information about what goes on after death:

> † **What is afterlife like? Is there a heaven? Have you seen God?**
>
> † **Are there really such beings as angels?**
>
> † **Can you give us the cure for cancer, AIDS, world hunger, war?**
>
> † **What about just a few lottery numbers?**

If asked, most ghost hunters would likely admit that their greatest ghost hunting dream is to *interview* a ghost in front of a video camera so the results could be shown on *World News* and tabloid programs, thereby bringing fame to the ghost hunter and proving to millions of people that ghosts positively exist.

Proof is the elusive gold we are seeking. Yet evidence is often of a personal nature.

Ghosts don't return from the grave to be interviewed. They have their own reasons for returning. We're just not privy to their agendas.

Most of the adult ghost hunters present on the investigation are well prepared for what may lay ahead. Most of the people who comprise this group have seen ghosts in their lifetimes. Probably all have witnessed manifestations of spirits. Such manifestations might include:

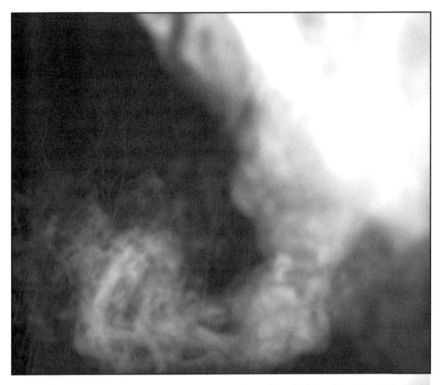

Are there apparitions forming in this ghostly mist at Pine Hollow Cemetery? *Photo by The Paranormal Adventurers.*

† hearing *spirit knocking* on walls or feeling or hearing the footfalls of an invisible walking down a hallway in a house;

† seeing *objects moving* seemingly of their own accord or orbs flying across rooms or shooting up staircases;

† spotting the blank faces of dead people in mirrors or *mists materializing* where none belong;

† receiving recurring telephone calls from a non-caller or perceiving ghostly images in television screens;

† watching electronics turn on or off by themselves; and the smell cigarette, cigar, or pipe smoke.

Perhaps they might have smelled the scent of perfume once worn by somebody who has died or maybe they smelled pleasant scents of apple pies baking, or of flowers, such as roses.

Maybe they felt things like cold winds rush by them while watching television or they had been touched on the head, shoulder, face, or hands.

Possibly they heard murmuring in their rooms as they lay in bed, or had blankets yanked off them when no one else was in the room, or seen a full bodied apparition appear in a doorway, hallway, or on a staircase, or at the foot of their bed in the middle of the night.

Maybe they were woken up by a ghost who whispered in their ears while they slept. Perhaps they woke up only to find a ghost leaning down beside them when they opened their eyes.

‡‡‡‡‡‡‡‡‡

Erica was in charge of the investigation. She put it together and it would be her directions we would follow. After all, she was the one who saw the ghost that brought us here in the first place. Erica is not a taskmaster, but she will steer people when needed.

Almost immediately we started to congregate on the small hill where Erica saw the ghost of the man in all black. Many of us quickly began setting up still or video cameras and talking to each other about our equipment or about the investigations we have been on lately. Some started snapping pictures right away.

Typically, P.A.S.T. investigations are relaxed with little structure because too many people attend them to coordinate duties within the few hours we have to investigate a site. Some members of P.A.S.T. also belong to different paranormal clubs. These other clubs are smaller and more in-depth, wherein members might be assigned specific duties on investigations in accordance with a predetermined methodology.

P.A.S.T., on the other hand, like most other paranormal groups on Long Island, includes members ranging from the novice to the

expert. Some groups are more for experts only. Sometimes these expert groups require in-house training of investigators. These groups may also demand much time from members and possibly financial contributions, but they also offer rewarding investigations to their members.

For the first free-flowing hour, the investigators at Pine Hollow would, at times, wander from the hill and spend time studying something curious that somebody noticed in an area of the graveyard away from the hill. People photographed graves in every part of the cemetery, exploring the possibilities of spirits appearing in these spots. Flashes would unexpectedly light sections of the cemetery, flooding a large area of graves with a bright light for just a fraction of a second. Small groups of four or five people would then stand together studying the screens of their cameras. I stood in one of these groups after I had taken photos of paranormals mists around the granddaddy pine tree. Others photographed orbs over the graves near the far end of the cemetery where the night is the darkest.

Diane had wandered off by herself among the graves. I could see her bent over a grave talking to the spirit of the person buried within in an effort to make contact. She was armed only with a Canon digital camera.

It's Diane's habit to stay to herself while investigating a graveyard. She is an **empathic**, which means that she picks up on feelings of the dead. An empathic is not to be confused with a psychic. As a rule she does not see images or get messages from deceased people the way psychics do. She *feels* things. As a Reiki practitioner, she is sensitive to energy. As an empathic, she is sensitive to lingering emotions.

The most extraordinary example of Diane's empathic abilities was displayed several years ago when she felt the feelings of Sally Townsend who lived in Raynham Hall in Oyster Bay during the American Revolution. As an investigation ensued in the old house that is now a museum, Diane increasingly felt the sadness Sally felt over the separation between herself and a young British officer who had gone back to England after the two fell in love.

The couple had met when British soldiers took over her family's home during the occupation of Long Island.

Diane wept and sobbed uncontrollably as she stood by a window looking out in the direction towards the bay on this particular day when we investigated Raynham Hall. A psychic who walked in on her while she was alone in a room in the old house said she saw not Diane, but a young woman in colonial clothing upon entering the room.

Most times Diane does not get feelings when in a graveyard, but when she does I pay attention to her. Tonight she did not report anything extraordinary.

‡‡‡‡‡‡‡‡‡

I was getting an unusually high number of mists at the old granddaddy pine tree. Some of the other ghost hunters thought it was odd that I was capturing so much activity.

Thick paranormal mist forming around the haunted tree.
Photo by The Paranormal Adventurers.

They stood there watching me. They would look at my camera and then they would take a picture with their own cameras and then look back at mine and see that there was no comparison. In most cases, my camera was catching images their cameras did not catch.

I was also a bit confused as to the reason the spirits where showing themselves to me. I wanted to chalk it up to how good I was as an investigator, but I knew it had nothing to do with me, and the other investigators present knew this, too.

They'd look at the two-inch screen on the back of my camera and say, "Wow, look at that mist! Why am I not getting that in my camera?"

I had no answer for them. I didn't understand what the spirits were up to until later than night when I realized they wanted one witness who would document the dramatic events that were to unfold.

As we milled around the granddaddy pine tree, the small cluster of people I was among suddenly got wind of murmurings that something extraordinary was going on with Erica at the hill. This might be the moment many of us had hoped would occur. Most of us immediately forgot what we were doing and went to the hill to see what was going on. The cemetery is not more than a few acres big, so getting to the hill was only a matter of thirty seconds at most.

"Erica's *talking* to the spirit," somebody in the shadows said as I approached the hill.

When we arrived, we learned Erica had just finished challenging the spirit of the hill. "You showed yourself and scared the hell out of me when I was alone," she said to the hill, intending for the words to reach the invisible spirit of the man she had seen there. "You're not so brave now that my friends are here with me."

No sooner had the words left Erica's lips than witnesses saw her eyes widen as she stared intently at something up on the hill. It was apparent that only she saw whatever it was she was watching.

"Look at that bright light!" she then blurted.

The investigators searched the hill, but they didn't see a bright light. "What bright light?" they asked as they clamored around Erica, searching her dark eyes for meaning.

"That orb on the hill!" she exclaimed, pointing at it. "It's right there!"

Everyone looked, but there was nothing out of the ordinary to see on the hill. The ghost hunters around her gaped incredulously back at her with questioning faces.

Erica quickly lifted the camera she held in her hand and took a picture of the orb she was seeing. Immediately appearing on the screen at the back of her camera was the image of a bright, oddly shaped orb. It was shaped like a dewdrop.

"THIS is what I saw," she stated, looking from one baffled investigator to another. *(Visit www.paranormaladventurers.com to see Erica's orb photograph and other photos from the night.)*

Fellow ghost hunters were now aware that Erica had been visited, or at least saw a light anomaly nobody else saw. The "visitation" was for her alone.

Excitement on the hill suddenly swelled like the discordant music of an orchestra tuning up—and a swift moving symphony was about to start.

To the faces searching for an explanation to the mysterious appearance of the orb, Erica could only explain that the likeness of the orb she had captured in the photo was an exact match to the orb she had seen with her naked eyes. She described it as being about two feet in diameter, though it was not perfectly round.

If there was any one spot in the night where I would say all hell had broken loose, it would be at this point. This is the moment everything started to change — *when the spirits came out to play.*

The symphony had started.

The "Misthaunt"

Like the others on the hill, I was now aware that the spirits were around. Diane was still at another part of the graveyard, but I could feel a certain heaviness in my chest that comes to me only when spirits are present. It's a telltale sign to me that something paranormal is about to happen. It's like knowing a storm is about to rage from the distant rumblings of thunder and the dark clouds on the horizon.

The first photo I shot of the hill was of the area where the orb had appeared to Erica. I did this immediately following my study of Erica's photo of the orb on her camera screen. Only a mere minute had passed since the whole orb visitation. A palpable tension hung in the air now in anticipation of the spirit showing itself to the whole group.

When I looked at my camera to see if I caught anything unusual in the photograph, I saw there was, in fact, nothing out of the ordinary in the photo. No orb, nothing. It was just a picture of a few gravestones and some trees at the top of a dark hill.

Next, I took a photo of Erica on the hill. When I shot the photo, I saw in the light of the camera's flash a large white blob, like a white sheet, spread out before Erica's body. I thrilled in anticipation as I looked at my camera screen after taking this photo because I knew it would reveal a mist covering Erica just like I had seen with my naked eyes in the camera's flash! And there it was, as I knew it would be! Mists can usually be spotted in the light of the camera's flash.

I gazed at the mist over Erica in the picture, suddenly perplexed by what I saw because the mist seemed to cover a wide sweep of the hill whereupon Erica stood, yet the photo I had taken only a few seconds before had not shown any mist on the hill.

I took another photograph to see if there was any of this mist lingering on the hill. Erica was not in this photograph. The result was that there was no mist in the photograph. The camera screen revealed mere graves and some trees at the top of a hill.

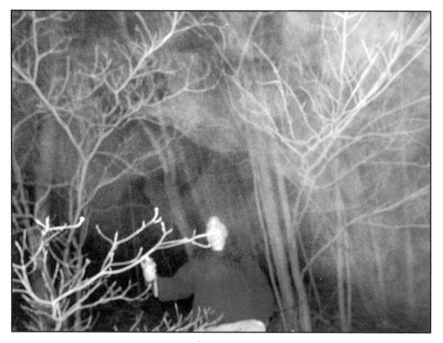

Paranormal investigator Erica Popino surrounded by ghostly mist on the haunted hill where the ghost of a man dressed in all black appeared to her.
Photo by The Paranormal Adventurers.

I aimed the camera back at Erica as she walked on the hill and snapped another photograph. In the light of the camera's flash, my eyes again caught the white shape of a mist. The photograph was again blurred by the camera focusing on the mist it saw rather than Erica. However, this time the mist appeared *beside* Erica. I looked down at the screen on the back of the large black Sony camera in my hand and I saw a large mist looming beside Erica. It was a thick white mist, not at all like the mist created by released breath. It was more the kind of misty substance that was referred to as *ectoplasm* in the days of the Spiritualist movement a hundred and fifty years ago.

As I gazed upon the photograph, I was struck by the fact that the mist had the appearance of leaning or moving towards Erica—as if IT was *watching* her. It seemed that the mist had a personality of its own and that this personality was aiming itself at Erica. It seemed to be leaning towards her, scrutinizing her.

Mist pursues paranormal investigator Erica Popino on the cemetery's haunted hill. *Photo by The Paranormal Adventurers.*

I didn't say anything to anybody at this point because I wanted to solve this mystery with my own logic. "Why is this mist only around Erica?" I wondered.

I took a picture of a different person on the hill in an effort to see if the mist would repeat itself. There was no mist in the resultant photo. So far, the mist only showed itself around Erica.

Then I leveled the camera at Erica again as she stood on the hill and my finger snapped off another shot. I soon saw that a mist still loomed above Erica's head, off to the side. It floated five feet above her. What's more, I had seen the shape of the mist in the light of the camera's flash and it appeared to have a large body, but I could not discern what the shape resembled, if anything. Only a small part of this mist shows in the photograph.

I knew at this point I was onto something. Through experimentation I had at least developed a working hypothesis that a spirit in the form of a mist was *moving* beside, above,

The mist of the haunted hill leans toward Erica Popino during a group investigation. *Photo by The Paranormal Adventurers.*

and around Erica. Had she conjured the ghost of Pine Hollow Cemetery through her provocation? Was it now manifesting as a mist instead of an apparition? If so, why?

It dawned on me that either my camera had the ability to catch the images of the mists following Erica around, or the spirit was specifically revealing itself to my camera for its own reasons. I would tuck this thought into the file cabinet in the back of my mind for later examination. The mist, of course, seemed to be purposely showing itself to me and nobody else, much like the mists around the old granddaddy pine tree across the cemetery. People had captured mists that evening, but nobody was capturing them at this particular time and at this particular spot, as far as I could tell. Was this directly the result of Erica calling upon the ghost of the hill?

I have since developed the theory that the spirit wanted to show Erica that it was around her and it picked one person to do the task

of recording the images as a testimony of its presence. Perhaps I was picked because the camera I was using was more advanced than the other cameras being used, or maybe because Erica trusted me to deliver an accurate assessment of the events that took place. After all, I had been a newspaper reporter for many years. Maybe the spirit sensed this, too. Maybe I was the one who was appointed to figure out what was going on, possibly so that some day I could write a book about it to let others know that spirits that want to make themselves known haunt Pine Hollow Cemetery. Again, the mystery of the other side leads us down one dark road after another and to more mysteries.

At this point I felt it was necessary to draw Erica's attention to the matter.

"Look, Erica," I said, "there is a mist following you."

She glanced down at my camera screen. All the mist photographs I had taken showed her standing or walking on the hill.

She turned away from me and went up the hill. She stopped in the center. "Take another photograph," she instructed.

The other investigators on the hill grew quiet. They were listening and observing the exchange between Erica and me.

The symphony had suddenly gone low for the moment, but the music was ever more intense with the violins frantic and a cello plucking piercing notes.

I took a photo of Erica. I saw the white shape of the large mist in the light of the camera flash. This is what I had seen in all the other photographs I had taken of her on the hill after she challenged the ghost and photographed the glowing orb that only she could see.

When I next looked down at the screen, I saw the familiar ghostly mist again hovering five feet above her head. Its image again filled me with the sense that it was a spirit gazing down at her. The photo was blurred because the mist appeared in front of Erica's image and the camera was focusing on the mist, not Erica.

Author Joseph Flammer, of *The Paranormal Adventurers*, repeatedly photographed the mist of the graveyard pursuing Erica Popino.
Photo by The Paranormal Adventurers.

"Here," I said. "See for yourself. Every photograph I'm taking of you has this mist in it!"

The look in Erica's brown eyes confirmed for me that she realized a spirit, manifesting as a mist, was following her around the hill. She lifted her own camera and photographed the night. When she studied her camera's screen she saw that she had captured nothing unusual, especially not a paranormal mist that was following only her.

The night suddenly filled with bright flashes. Everyone else with a camera worked in a frenzy to capture the ghostly mist around Erica. As far as I could ascertain, nobody was getting what I was getting in my camera.

I believed at that point that I had been *assigned* by the spirit the task of documenting the event for Erica's enlightenment. I didn't know why. To me it was as if the spirit was saying, "*See,*

if I want to I can be around you, Erica. Don't push me! I can be wherever you are, just for you." The thought was somewhat disconcerting, for had the spirit the ability to visit Erica at home? I dared not bring up the subject.

I continued to photograph Erica. In the light of the flash of each and every photo I took was the changing shape of a thick white mist. The mist was absent in photographs taken by the other investigators.

The sixteen members of the ghost investigation team were now fully absorbed in the matter unfolding on the hill, each one realizing they were witnessing a paranormal event the likes of which they might never see again.

Erica's voice trembled in response when I asked her whether or not she could see the white blob of the mist appearing in my camera's flash.

"I can't see anything," she said. Her voice was thin and quivering now.

She was wired, walking a tightrope, delighted the spirit appeared only to her, and dreading she alone was at the center of a storm taking place on the hill where she had seen a dead man's ghost only weeks before.

"You can't see that?" I asked excitedly. "You can't see that big white figure of the mist when my flash hits it?"

"No, I don't see anything," Erica repeated, turning excitedly around to see if she could spot anything behind her with her naked eyes.

To anybody else it might have sounded like Erica and I were arguing because our voices were raised. The truth is we were exhilarated because we knew, as everyone else present knew, we were in the midst of a paranormal happening. A supernatural event was taking place here. Such happenings are few and far between for most ghost investigators.

The most accurate description I could give to the occurrence was that it was not quite a haunting — wherein a ghost, like the man in black, appears — and it was not quite just the appearance

of mists in photographs. It was a combination of the two. I had once met an investigator at a haunted mansion in Massachusetts who called such an event a *misthaunt*.

Erica was the subject of the spirit's attention, of that we were sure; and I was to document the event so Erica could see that the spirit was specifically focused on *her*. The gravity of the possible ramifications according to this line of thinking was frightening to me. Was the spirit being friendly or hostile to Erica?

While this was going on, Mike Salvia, who in my and Diane's opinion, is hands down the best ghost videographer and spirit photographer on Long Island, was recording on video the events as they took place. He had Erica in the focus of his Sony Handicam. The camera was set on Nightshot and he used an infrared illuminator that he had attached to the top of the camera.

"I know it's not my breath," said Erica of the recurring mist.

She dropped to her knees on the hill and looked around. I took a photograph of her as she knelt there. Again, a shape appeared in the light of the camera flash. The mist was high above her head. The image instantly appeared on the camera's screen, too.

I showed Erica the photo I had just snapped.

"Okay, I'm going to cover my mouth and not breathe," she said.

She sat on the ground and covered her mouth and her nostrils with her sweater so she could not create a mist by expelling breath.

I took a photo.

Again, a repeat of what I had taken so many times already: the mist appeared in the flash and high above Erica's head in the subsequent photograph.

I showed Erica the picture.

"I wasn't even breathing!" she exclaimed. "It couldn't have been my breath! I wasn't even breathing!"

Now the deep drums of a primordial music were added to the symphony. From the high balcony of our imaginations raged wild and clashing riffs of angelic voices without musical scores to follow, left to their own wanderings, like our thoughts raging in confusion upon that haunted hill.

Erica Popino (bottom of photograph) covers her nose and mouth with her sweatshirt to prove it is not her breath creating the manifestation on the hill.
Photo by The Paranormal Adventurers.

"Of course not," I said to Erica. "Of course you didn't create the mist! It's at least six feet away from you!"

"Boom! Boom. Boom!" beat the tense drums of the night.

The other investigators on the hill stood close together in mystified silence. Like Erica and I, they sought a reasonable explanation for the goings on with the mist. They looked around at the night wondering if the spirit was around them.

"Get out! Get out while you can!" the crows had cawed.

"Boom! Boom! Boom!" beat the drums.

"Erica, speak to the spirits some more!" I encouraged.

Erica faced the trees at the top of the hill. The music of the night suddenly hushed. The angels in the choir silenced.

"I wish you'd show yourself to us as the bright ball of light I saw," Erica implored. She spoke to the thin air of the elusive spirit of the hill.

I snapped a new photograph. The resultant image was of a mist high above Erica's head, just like all the others.

"Boom! Boom! Boom!"

"Who else can talk to the spirits?" I asked, turning to the ghost hunters standing behind me. The music of the night swooped and danced with skeletons around them. They searched for signs of ghosts.

"Who here is a psychic?" I asked.

Eighteen-year-old psychic Cyndi Philbin from Kings Park stepped forward. I was glad she stepped up to the plate because *now* is the time to connect with the ghosts, *now* is the time to reach the spirits, *now* is when we need answers.

"Okay, Cyndi," I said, "talk to the spirits."

Cyndi smiled and with her hands in her pockets began to quietly talk to the spirits. When I photographed her, she now also had a mist in front of her...but it did not stay long in front of her.

Psychic and paranormal investigator Cyndi Philbin surrounded by mists after she attempted to contact the spirit on the hill. *Photo by The Paranormal Adventurers.*

IT was on the move. In a second it would be back with Erica. Was it just inspecting this new person who was talking to it?

Another investigator, meanwhile, came forward on the hill. She had been snapping photographs earlier, but now used only her eyes to observe the environment. She had a small book bag slung over her shoulder.

Erica remained on the ground, searching the top of the hill. Cyndi sat on the ground, too, and talked to the spirits. The lady with the book bag searched the night with her naked eyes. The ghost hunters stood together taking photographs, hoping to see a spirit manifest.

I took a photograph amid this fever pitch. In the video Salvia shot that night the flash of my camera is clearly discernable at that minute. Immediately following I say, "Here he is again." I walk forward to Erica and show her the photo of the mist. In it, we can see the top of her head and the investigator with the

Erica Popino (bottom of photograph) is joined by another investigator as the spirit on the hill manifests above them. *Photo by The Paranormal Adventurers.*

Even as the night's investigation is concluding the spirit mist follows Erica Popino as she leaves the haunted hill with sensitive and paranormal investigator Karen Isaksen and another member of the team. *Photo by The Paranormal Adventurers.*

book bag slung over her shoulder. Up in the left hand corner of the photo is the familiar mist of the spirit manifesting for Erica's enlightenment. Again it appears to be looking down at her. Again, from this photo it is very clear that the mist is not the result of breath expelled from Erica's mouth.

Right about this time five investigators gathered together as one and tried to create a mist by exhaling breath in unison as I photographed their effort. We tried this twice. In neither attempt could they create a mist with their expelled breaths. They would breathe out and I would snap the shot and show them the results right away as evidence that the photo was in no way tampered with.

It wasn't until weeks later when Salvia gave me the video he shot that night of the interaction between the spirit and Popino on the hill that I actually spotted a mist moving around the cemetery

of its own accord. This mist moves quickly. It's not a mist released from somebody's breath. It appears to my right side as I'm talking to Erica. In fact, it's the very mist that I was detecting with my still camera throughout the night...the very one *following* Erica around the hill.

When Diane and I slowed Salvia's video down frame by frame at our studio, we suddenly saw that a face appears in this mist. It's a face with an open mouth, mangled teeth, and rotted out nose and eyes. A psychic told us the face is laughing at us as we chase it around the hill. It was having fun with us. You can view this video and see the mist and the face inside it on our website www.paranormaladventurers.com.

‡‡‡‡‡‡‡‡‡

The symphony has concluded. For the moment the drums are at rest. The plucking cello has ceased, waiting for the next audience to arrive.

Pine Hollow Cemetery is waiting to be understood. Be careful. Don't underestimate the spirits there.

Sweet Hollow Road

Long Island's MOST Haunted Place

Sweet Hollow Road...a place of MANY dark legends.
Photo by The Paranormal Adventurers.

Location: Melville, New York

Description: Sweet Hollow Road is roughly two miles long. It's a serene country road that winds past a well-maintained cemetery and a quiet nature preserve, under a parkway overpass, past county parklands and stables, and into residential areas, some with old forgotten family cemeteries in their backyards. The road does not have shoulders. It can be a dangerous road, especially at night. If you're planning to visit the road, it might be wise to first visit during the day.

How to get there: Take the Long Island Expressway to Exit 49 North (Route 110 heading to Huntington). Locally, Route 110 is called Broad Hollow Road. Sweet Hollow Road intersects with Route 110 about a half-mile north of the Long Island Expressway on the left (west) side of the road. The Sweet Hollow Diner, with its red neon lights across its facade, is located on the west side of Route 110, just yards from Sweet Hollow Road, so if all else fails find the diner to find the road.

‡‡‡‡‡‡‡‡‡‡

The Legends

Phantom Horses

The Overpass on Sweet Hollow Road. *Photo by The Paranormal Adventurers.*

No place on Long Island has a darker reputation for ghosts than Sweet Hollow Road in Melville. In its way, Sweet Hollow *is* Long Island's Sleepy Hollow.

As might you might recall from American literature class, *The Legend of Sleepy Hollow* is the harvest season tale of rural upstate New York written by Washington Irving and published in 1820. In the short story, a headless horseman terrorizes a silly galoot of a schoolteacher named Ichabod Crane by chasing him through the woods of old Sleepy Hollow at night.

113

Long Island's Sweet Hollow doesn't have a headless horseman, but legends abound of phantom horses running wild in the night on Sweet Hollow Road.

Sweet Hollow Road is a narrow country road that cuts through the treed parklands and rustic residential areas of a hamlet called Melville once known as Sweet Hollow. It's a perfect setting for tales of ghosts and legends of witches. One murderer who was never caught thought it was also the perfect place to dump the body of his teenage murder victim in 1976; probably because the road is pitch black there at night, he thought nobody would see him—and nobody did.

Though these ghost horses of Sweet Hollow do not terrorize people the way the headless horseman terrorized Ichabod Crane, the apparitions are nonetheless mystifying to the people who see them.

Yet the ghost horses of Sweet Hollow Road are the *tamest* of the ghosts haunting this estranged country hollow. With its mournful graveyards, secretive woods, and a long black road of haunted mystery, old Sweet Hollow is a place with much paranormal personality. Some might even say it's a place reminiscent of old horror movies. Thus, tales of ghost horses are the gentlest introduction to a road whose dark story will get bumpier the farther along we go into its perplexing strangeness.

‡‡‡‡‡‡‡‡‡

Kathy Abrams, of Bethpage, encountered just such a phantasm in the middle of a snowy night when she and her friend were driving home by way of Sweet Hollow Road.

Abrams, a rider and horse lover, thought the phantom horse she spotted loose in the night was a living, breathing animal that had somehow escaped from one of the stables located in the hollow. After all, this is horse-riding country with trails crisscrossing the local woods. The last thing she suspected at the

time was that the animal she spotted standing all alone under an overpass was a ghost!

Abrams pulled her Ford Probe over to the snow-blanketed grass on the side of the road and turned off the engine. Her friend looked out the windshield at the horse without speaking. Abrams rolled down the window. The brittle cold night poured in. She shuddered. Out in the storm only the tops of the tall trees seemed to be catching the howling wind.

Stepping out of the car, Abrams was suddenly alone and enveloped by the haunted night.

She moved slowly as she stepped in the crunching snow to the back of her car to get rope. She didn't want to spook the horse.

From the back of her car, she got the rope she needed to tie around the horse's neck. She shut the hatch gingerly and proceeded onto the road.

As she prepared herself to approach the animal, she looked around at the snowy night and wondered if any of the ghost stories she had heard about Sweet Hollow Road were true. There were so many!

The snow crunched under her feet. Great cold jets of mists flared out in front of her and flew upwards, dissipating into the nothingness of the night in a flash. Abrams caught herself remembering what a friend had told her about the ghosts that dwell in an old Indian burial ground in the woods of the hollow. She shivered back the thought as she pulled her heavy winter coat tighter around her neck and glanced at shadows at the edge of the woods.

Trees swayed and bobbed in the lone streetlight on the corner of Gwynne Road and Sweet Hollow Road. The light cast a hollow pall through the whirling snowflakes. Ironically, earlier in the night, before the snow came down heavily, a full moon beamed over the land.

Abrams recalled stories that said the ghosts of Sweet Hollow Road come out on full-moon nights.

She shook her head at her juvenile thoughts. She was all grown up now. She was eighteen. Childish stories should be left behind. She lifted her eyes to the whirling snowflakes that clouded the night. The horse had not moved. It watched her slowly approaching.

Abrams' plan was to place the rope she had gotten from her vehicle around the horse's neck and then walk the animal to a safe place. She wasn't afraid of the big creature. She loved horses. Years later she would even own a horse named *Lady*, an appaloosa.

She figured she'd bring the confused creature to the county stable located in parklands farther up Sweet Hollow Road. Once there, she aimed to tie the animal to the fence at a place where the horse would be out of harms way till someone found it in the morning and took it inside the stable for food and warmth.

Abrams remembered the horse as Diane and I interviewed her at the exact location where she witnessed the apparition on Sweet Hollow Road. With our video camera trained on her, she recalled:

> "He was standing there alone...you could see the steam coming out of his nostrils. You could hear him breathing..."

But as Abrams drew close, the horse suddenly spooked and bolted away, leaving clouds of its breath behind to vanish into the air.

The great horse ran northward a short distance to Gwynne Road, a dead end road that intersects with Sweet Hollow only a few hundred feet north of the dark and dingy overpass where the horse had sought protection from the night.

Tonight, in the snowfall and hollow light, the dead end took on the surreal aspect of a Hollywood movie set. Long shadows danced in the crying winds, bobbing amid the dull pallor of the single streetlight on the corner of Gwynne.

The ghost horse hoofed up Gwynne Road and jumped a low gate at the dead end. It then vanished into snowy oblivion of the forever unknown where ghost horses go after they are done haunting people.

Abrams was startled. But even at that point she still had not realized she had just seen a ghost.

Only when she looked down at the pristine snow in the half-light of the snowstorm did her eyes scan and access the evidence that registered the fact in her brain that a piece of the night's puzzle was missing. Looking down at the snow she realized instantly that something far stranger than a mere horse alone in the night was wrong here: something paranormal was happening! The slight of hand of ghosts was at work here!

She blinked and refocused her eyes and then looked all around, turning her body in a complete circle so she could see everywhere she had walked and everywhere the horse had run. What she saw was only her footprints in the snow and the nearby tire tracks of her car.

"There were no hoof prints in the snow," Abrams explained. "Even back at the area where we saw him standing under the overpass, there were no hoof prints. He was just *NOT* there!"

‡‡‡‡‡‡‡‡‡

Then there's the case of the woman who attended one of our lectures. She told us of her experience with the phantom horse of Sweet Hollow Road.

"I saw it with my own eyes!" the woman insisted. "It just disappeared!"

The lady looked around the room. People stared back at her with opened mouths. Some who knew the secrets of Sweet Hollow Road nodded to her in affirmation, reflecting on their own experiences. "It just up and disappeared!" she repeated. "Vanished! Poof!"

When asked, the woman said she knew nothing of Abrams' experience.

And there have been other people, too, who never heard Abrams' story, yet claim to have seen ghost horses with their own eyes in the mysterious hollow.

Mike Salvia, a paranormal investigator from Old Bethpage, told us of the ghostly experience he had one strange night on Sweet Hollow Road. During an encounter with the spirits of the road, he caught the image of a ghost horse in his digital camera. *(Visit www.paranormaladventurers.com to see Salvia's photos.)*

Salvia said he and a female friend went to Sweet Hollow Road one July night to conduct ghost photography. He was photographing outside the imposing black wrought iron gates of Melville Cemetery on Sweet Hollow Road in the dark of the night when a white mist formed right in front of him. As he watched, the mist took on the shape of what he described as "one big apparition."

Salvia, a seasoned ghost investigator, is known in the Long Island paranormal community for his outstanding ghost photography, video, and EVP (electronic voice phenomenon). He has seen ghosts on many occasions and is well-versed in the slight of hand of spirits. So on this night on Sweet Hollow Road, when a ghost paid him a visit, he was ready.

"I had my camera and I photographed it," Salvia said.

Diane and I were sitting in his apartment in Old Bethpage as he told us his story. The night seemed to close in on us as we listened to his words.

"There it is," he pointed.

On the computer screen before us was the image of a mist, and in the right hand corner of the photo Salvia had inserted a computer drawn sketch of what he thinks he photographed in the mist. In fact, what he believes he caught was a horse's head with the image of a person beside it, "possibly an Indian," he said. At the top of the photo in red letters he wrote, "This is what I see." And at the bottom of the sketch he wrote, "In the Melville Cemetery."

Salvia explained the image of the ghost horse was so striking to him that he felt compelled to draw a picture of what he believed he saw in the mist so others could compare the two images and judge for themselves.

The photograph of the horse head in the mist was the last photo in a long line of extraordinary photographs Salvia showed us that night as we interviewed him for our DVD, "The Ghosts of Sweet Hollow Road," which was released in the fall of 2009 and is available on our website.

Just before he showed us the image of the ghost horse, Salvia had summoned to his computer screen the image of a mist that seemed to be taking on the shape of a person floating gracefully through the air. This photograph was taken within moments of the horse head photo. This photo, too, can be viewed on our website.

The stage was set for Salvia's night of phantom horses, ghostly mists, and apparitions on Sweet Hollow Road when he noticed that orbs were taking over his photographs. This took place when he photographed the landscape of Melville Cemetery.

The concentrations of orbs were at times so heavy in the photographs they obliterated the very scenery of the graveyard. Salvia said he shot these photos by holding the camera between the cold, black, wrought iron bars of the cemetery's front gate. He shot through the gate and not actually inside because the cemetery was closed and it's illegal to enter the property at night.

A clear photo of a road in the graveyard, a utility pole, and a light shining towards the camera from the back of the cemetery all but vanish in subsequent photos shot during this wild orb fest. When the orbs visited Salvia, the road was hardly visible. The light at the back of the cemetery was mostly obliterated. The utility pole that is so evident in the prior shot simply disappeared! See the difference between the before and after photographs by visiting Salvia's photographs on our website. Exclaimed Salvia:

"If each orb is a spirit — and there are over a hundred thousand orbs here — then this is like a concert in Saratoga in the middle of July on a back road on Long Island!"

> "And I believe in orbs," he went on, drawing a difference between dust orbs and orbs that are spirit. "I had interactions with orbs — with *spirit orbs*.
>
> "As for saying whether these are spirit orbs," continued Salvia, "all I know is that I've experienced paranormal activity on Sweet Hollow Road and these are orbs on Sweet Hollow Road and they don't appear to this camera at any other time than on this night."

Salvia said that after he downloaded the digital images on his computer and viewed the mists on a monitor, he was certain spirits had *visited* him on Sweet Hollow Road the night he caught the images.

There is clearly enough detail in the mist to see where Salvia got the idea he had captured a ghost horse in the mists. Likewise, after viewing his other photos on our website, you will also see how he would arrive at the conclusion that he was haunted that night.

Was a ghost horse really in the mist? Given Sweet Hollow Road's reputation — even in the area of ghost horses — one would have to say it very well could have been the apparition of a horse that Salvia caught.

The Overpass

Unlike Salvia's story of the mists at Melville Cemetery, Abrams' experience with the ghost horse in the snowy night took place at the infamous Northern State Parkway overpass. The overpass crosses Sweet Hollow Road in a wooded area located only about a half-mile north of Melville Cemetery.

The phantom horse that Abrams saw appeared to be taking shelter from the snowfall in the dark tunnel underneath the overpass. As ghost hunters, we have to ask:

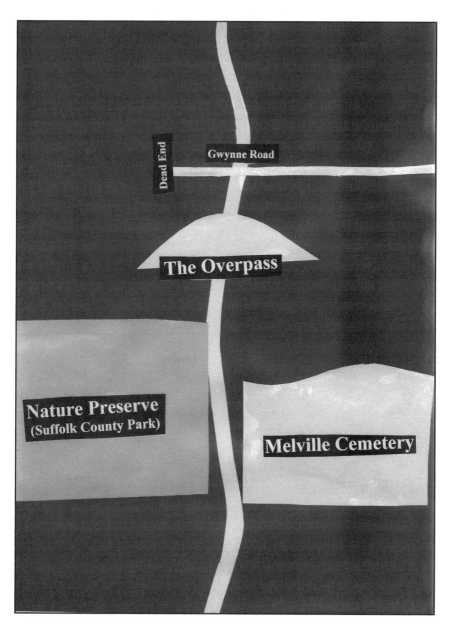

Author Joseph Flammer has drawn a map of the most haunted part of Sweet Hollow Road.

† Why would a ghost horse be taking shelter from falling snow? After all, ghosts can't feel the snow, can they?

† How can they feel cold if they don't even have real bodies?

† Aren't ghosts known for being *disembodied*?

The answers as to why the ghost horse sought shelter from the storm eludes us, for ghosts are literally shadows of the beings they once were, *not* physical beings of this world. But ghosts are often reported doing things we wouldn't suspect they would be doing.

We have heard a first-hand story from Gloria, of Wantagh, that is as perplexing in its details as the story of the ghost horse that sought shelter under the overpass.

Gloria, whose story we documented for our upcoming book, *Long Island Love Stories from Beyond*, said the ghost of her husband Jack appeared to her on the very night of his cremation. He had collapsed and died a few days earlier while sitting on a stool in the family den. She showed us the very spot where he died and hung her head as she told us how he appeared to her as a ghost on the night he was put to rest.

Gloria recalled being fully awake and sitting up in bed in her well-lighted bedroom, "feeling sad."

Suddenly, her husband's ghost appeared to her.

"Jack walked in the room," Gloria recalled. "I was in total shock!"

Jack leaned towards Gloria. He looked into her eyes. He gave her a kiss. Gloria *felt* his lips upon her own.

Then the ghost of her husband pointed to his watch and said, "I don't have much time."

"No, Jack, stay!" Gloria called out to her husband's ghost.

"I don't have much time," he said again. "I love you."

"And with that he just walked out," said Gloria. "He didn't disappear...he just walked out and the image grew fainter."

An obvious question that any good ghost hunter would have to be wondering right about now is:

Why is a ghost wearing a watch? Do ghosts keep a daily schedule in the afterlife? Are there clocks on the walls on the *other side*? Do spirits function according to a twenty-four hour schedule like humans on planet Earth?

Or, do ghosts *think* they are still in the world? Are they trapped in a delusion that they are still alive? Do they even know they are dead?

Here's another confusing case: A woman in one of our audiences at a library told us she saw her aunt walking across her backyard as the children played in the pool on a hot summer day. The aunt, whom the woman did not know had died earlier that day, was carrying a Big Gulp soda from a 7-11 convenience store.

Again, we have to ask: What is a ghost doing with a Big Gulp soda?

Likewise, why would a ghost horse on Sweet Hollow Road try to avoid falling snow?

Of course, the answer is: we don't know. We can only guess.

The fact is we don't understand ghosts.

The popular theory about ghosts is that they are the shades of people who died suddenly, usually tragically, the results of accidents, murder, or maybe even war as in the case at Gettysburg, Pennsylvania. In Gettysburg, 51,000 casualties were recorded during a three-day battle in 1863. Today many people claim they see and hear the ghosts of soldiers who think they are still in battle.

There is no doctorate program for ghost hunters. We ghost investigators stumble our way through the dark of the unknown with what we can gather from reports and glean through our own investigations.

The ghosts of animals are just as baffling to us as the ghosts of humans. We suspect they appear to us because they have some unfinished business here on Earth, too — just like the ghosts of people.

Not always does the appearance of a ghost make sense.

Many times the people who witness ghosts find no relevance or connection between the spirit and themselves.

Take for example the retired New York State Supreme Court judge that one night stood up at one of our lectures in the Southold Public Library and walked to the front of the room to tell a story of how the ghost of a man appeared to him and his son as they were talking in the upstairs hallway in their home in Garden City. The ghost, whom neither he nor his son recognized, walked through the hallway and through a wall, vanishing just as quickly as it had appeared. The judge told the story as his wife nodded in agreement with her husband from her seat. If you can't believe a judge, whom can you believe?

The Haunted Mile

Though cars are rarely seen passing over Sweet Hollow Road by means of the ominous overpass, the screams of their whirling tires on the hard pavement can be heard as they zip through the area.

Each day the arched stone overpass contributes its part in carrying many thousands of Long Islanders along the Northern State Parkway to points east and west on Long Island.

The overpass, as it's referred to by ghost hunters, is located about a mile up Sweet Hollow Road as one travels northward from Route 110, and this is the reason this portion of the road is sometimes referred to as the *haunted mile*.

After turning onto Sweet Hollow Road from Route 110 drivers must first cross Old Country Road. This is a simple and historic road that intersects with Sweet Hollow Road.

Then, to continue to the overpass, drivers must pass the black gates of the Melville Cemetery on the right side of the road and then navigate into the woods of the West Hills Nature Preserve, a Suffolk County park, whose eerie trees loom from both sides of the narrow road like monsters ready to reach out and grab people up as they pass by.

This stretch of road from the graveyard to the overpass — about a quarter-mile distance — is the most haunted section of the *haunted mile.*

The Suicide Teens

Many frightening stories and legends circulate concerning the *haunted mile.*

The Overpass—where it's said three teenagers hanged themselves in a suicide pact. *Courtesy of Karen Isaksen.*

125

Perhaps the most notorious of the stories is about three teenagers who killed themselves by hanging from the overpass in the mid-1970s as part of a suicide pact. Legends connected to this dark event say that if drivers shift their vehicles into neutral under the overpass, the vehicles will roll uphill by themselves as if pushed by the spirits of the dead teenagers.

Many people swear ghostly handprints appear on their vehicles as they are rolled backward or forward when inside the dark tunnel.

One woman in our audience at a library lecture claimed she sprinkled white powder on the trunk of her car before driving slowly into the overpass and placing the vehicle in neutral. Inside the tunnel a force she could not see pushed the car. When she drove out and inspected the white powder, she found the impression of a hand in it.

A different woman we interviewed on video swore that a handprint appeared on the back window of her car while she was in the tunnel. Not only did she see it, but so did her two daughters whose testimonies we also recorded.

It might actually be gravity that is responsible for making cars move. The road slants ever so slightly under the overpass.

But many people we have spoken with insist their vehicles moved in the direction opposite the pull of gravity. In other words, something pushed them or pulled them *uphill*. This report is so common and so widespread that to dispute it would be futile.

Diane and I have experimented many times by parking under the overpass and setting the shifter in neutral; the car never moved against gravity for us.

This is not to say that it couldn't happen. A woman I spoke with told me she had actually been pushed *UP* the stairs at the Country House Restaurant in Stony Brook many years ago by an unseen entity. The woman said she was delivering a cake for a bakery at the time. The cake was for an important affair at the restaurant that day. As she was walking up the steps of the staircase she was suddenly shoved hard forwards. The cake crashed to the

Mysteries dwell inside the Overpass. *Photo by The Paranormal Adventurers.*

ground. The woman had to explain that a ghost pushed her *up* the stairs. The manager blinked at her, she said.

If a woman can be pushed *up* the stairs at a restaurant, why can't a car be pushed up the slight incline of a slanting road?

Many folks blow their vehicles' horns as they approach the claustrophobic tunnel of the overpass — or sometimes while they're in it — responding to folklore that three beeps keep the ghosts of the teens from appearing with the suicide nooses around their necks and their feet kicking and bodies jerking in the air, as if they had only a second earlier dropped to their violent deaths. Other people we've spoken to say they beep their horns three times to make the ghosts appear. The meaning of the beeping depends on with whom you're speaking.

We have never met anyone who's actually seen the three hanging teenagers. However, we have met people who swore they saw black shadows moving about the area of the overpass. We have also seen these black shadows darting around the overpass,

so we agree with people who say shadow people move through day and the night on Sweet Hollow Road.

Many people also report hearing dreary music or murmuring voices under the overpass as they sit in the shadows of the tunnel waiting for ghosts, listening to the haunted night and the screaming tires from overhead. Some of these people claim they hear the voices of children crying.

Diane had such an experience one full-moon night in August 2007. She heard music *inside* the tunnel.

"It sounded like children's music," she reported that night.

After hearing the music, Diane stepped outside of the tunnel and looked up at the old stone bricks of the looming overpass. She heard the crying of tires on the road overhead and the cicadas buzzing their chaotic late summer songs in the woods, but no music. The music could only be heard *inside* the tunnel!

"The children are locked inside the tunnel," Diane realized, and she pointed the flashlight around at the graffiti on the dirty tunnel walls for the ghosts that sang to her.

A few years later in Barton, Vermont, located in the woods of the Northeast Kingdom not far from the Canadian border, Diane would hear the talking, songs, and shouts of a *talking* waterfall!

It's a waterfall where other people had heard the water talk too.

The owners of the property told us an Indian burial ground is located beside the waterfall. They reported tragedy on the site as their house was being built at the top of the falls, with one man losing the right side of his face from a chain that slipped off a rock cutter. "Do you think it's possible all this bad energy was actually the spirits telling us they didn't want us to build above the waterfall?" the owner asked me with an urgency in his voice when he visited our cabin one night during a rainstorm. His eyes leveled at mine.

"We don't subscribe to evil," I told him. "If a ghost is responsible for tragedy on your property, then I'd have to agree with you and say it was evil. But we don't believe ghosts are evil. It sounds to us like it was coincidence that the man was hurt and other things went wrong while you were building your house."

The owner of the house beside the waterfall looked away as if dreaming. "The man lost his eye and part of his face," he said. "And a lot of other bad things happened. The bridge we built washed away in the waterfall and we had to rebuild it."

Diane's experience with the children's music in the tunnel of the overpass on Sweet Hollow Road is not such a far cry from our experience in the four-mile long Hoosac Train Tunnel of North Adams, Massachusetts, which we investigated with members of the Berkshire Paranormal Group in 2007. We were in town to speak at a conference at the haunted Houghton Mansion on Church Street.

Two hundred men died while building the privately owned Hoosac train tunnel, fifty men for each mile of it that bores right though a mountain.

In the pitch-black night inside the stone tunnel we heard the ghosts of dead men screaming from deeper inside the hole. It sounded as if they were calling for help, some said. Moreover, we took the now famous photograph, "The Watchers," which captured the faces of two men on the stonewall of the infamous tunnel. The men were watching us. *(The photo is available for review on our website.)*

Of course, the legend of the suicide teens of Sweet Hollow Road's overpass is false. No teenagers ever hanged themselves from the overpass.

We know this because we interviewed Huntington Town's Historian Robert Hughes and Archivist Antonia Mattheou about this legend and both stated emphatically the legend is false.

Hughes and Mattheou also informed us that every other legend about the *haunted mile* of Sweet Hollow Road that we recited to them was false. We will discuss these other legends shortly.

What's more, we could not find any documentation or references to these supposed suicides or any of the other legends of the *haunted mile* when we researched newspapers, vertical files, and books at libraries.

Some of our research was conducted at the Half Hollow Hills Library, which is actually located on Sweet Hollow Road, only about a half-mile from the nature preserve, the epee-center of paranormal activity in the hollow. Surely, we thought, the Half Hollow Hills Library would have information about the suicide teenagers since the library maintains files on the history of Sweet Hollow, later to be named *Melville*, but it didn't. Nothing was ever written and filed away about the suicides.

The reason Half Hollow Hills Library and other libraries didn't have information about the suicide teens is because the deaths never took place.

This is not to say the overpass is not haunted. Too many people have had told us of their personal experiences at the overpass to dismiss out of hand. It just isn't haunted by "suicide teens," that's all.

Mary of Sweet Hollow Road—was she a killer? *Courtesy of Karen Isaksen.*

Mary

Hands down the most repeated story about Sweet Hollow Road, and perhaps the most frightening because of the dark shadows of the supernatural it casts into our reality, is that of the ghost of *Mary*.

While it seems nearly every town on Long Island has a story about the ghost of "Mary" or "Hatchet Mary," there is something far more sinister lurking in the visceral legends of Mary of Sweet Hollow Road.

According to the legends, Mary is a witch who killed children and adults in a horrific fire. Either she died by committing suicide — by burning to death with the kids after she locked herself and everyone else in the building — or she was hanged or maybe even burned at the stake by the townspeople for her wicked doings. These aspects of evil are missing in stories of Mary originating from other Long Island hamlets and are unique to Sweet Hollow Road.

131

The legend of Hatchet Mary is found in many hamlets on Long Island. *Courtesy of Karen Isaksen.*

When I was a child growing up in Oceanside in Nassau County, for example, I was thrilled on windy Halloween nights when the older boys and girls of the neighborhood sat on my front stoop and shared their half-baked stories about "Hatchet Mary." They claimed Mary butchered her husband with a hatchet in an old house located on a hill in Oceanside.

"Whack, the hatchet fell! Whack, the hatchet dug! Whack, the hatchet cut her husband's head clean off!"

The exact location in Oceanside of this house of horrors was always annoyingly foggy to me. Nobody ever brought me to the house to show me where all this mayhem occurred, though I

oftened asked the older boys to bring me there by riding bicycles to the spot.

What's more, nobody could tell me on what street the dark house on the hill with the bare trees out front was located.

Even at ten-years-old, some of the cloudy details of this *Hatchet Mary* story seemed too unlikely to me to be true, as I couldn't think of a single place in Oceanside where I had ever seen a hill! The land is absolutely flat in that part of Nassau County.

Of course, the story reeked of lies because it was false.

Variations of the same false story are still widespread in hamlets across Long Island. *Mary*, in these legends, is a vague horror fiction character whose crimes are regarded almost tongue-in-cheek as folklore, not fact. People who repeat these stories as local lure seem to know they are false, but overlook this detail in favor of perpetuating a good scary story about their community.

How people speak of the Mary legend of Sweet Hollow is vastly different than how people speak of her counterparts in other hamlets. The crimes she committed in Sweet Hollow were committed at a specific place, on Mt. Misery Road, and people who recite them, as if the stories are true, typically speak of the legends solemnly, perhaps even reverently. It's hard not to notice this trait after speaking with many people about these legends.

While the building Mary was said to have burned down doesn't exist anymore — because she *burned* it down — the woods in which the building stood and the road associated with her legends do exist. The woods can be hiked and the road driven. These places even lend themselves to investigations by paranormal enthusiasts. This difference alone sets the Mary legends of Sweet Hollow Road apart from Mary legends from other areas of Long Island where it's taken as more tongue-in-cheek by its citizenry than in Melville.

Simply put, there are more physical specifics to the Mary of Sweet Hollow legends than her counterparts in other communities.

But there is an even more glaring difference to note between the legends from Sweet Hollow and other locales: the types of crimes Mary was said to have committed are of an entirely different nature.

For instance, the witch of Sweet Hollow is said to have killed children by burning down a hospital or a school with the kids and employees locked inside. Like the main character of *Carrie* by Stephen King, Mary apparently locked all the doors in the building before she set fire at the exits so nobody could get out.

A variation of this legend says only Mary escaped the flames, but was soon hunted down and captured by an angry mob of the townspeople and burned at the stake in the woods on Mt. Misery. Some versions say she was hanged, not burned.

In contrast, the legends of "Mary" in most other towns say Mary killed her husband or her lover, or was killed by her husband or her lover. This is far tamer than the stories of Mary committing

Mary of Sweet Hollow Road was said to have burned down a school or a hospital on nearby Mt. Misery Road. Her ghost is believed to haunt the woods and roads surrounding Mt. Misery. *Courtesy of Karen Isaksen.*

suicide by burning down a school or a hospital full of screaming kids and adults.

In other towns, Mary committed murder. In Sweet Hollow, Mary committed a massacre!

The building Mary is said to have burned down — whether she was inside it or not — was supposed to have been located in woods situated on Mount Misery.

Even today visitors to this road at night claim they hear the screams of the ghosts of people who were trapped in the burning building.

Like Sweet Hollow Road, old Mt. Misery Road was just an Indian path in the woods before it was transformed into a road for horse-drawn wagons by whites who settled the area in force, probably around 1850. A person whom Diane and I spoke with who grew up in this location told us that these roads were not even paved until the 1950s.

Sweet Hollow and Mt. Misery Roads run parallel to each other, with Old Country Road running perpendicular and connecting both.

To visualize the relationship of the three local roads — Sweet Hollow Road, Old Country Road, and Mt. Misery Road — one must understand that they all border West Hills Nature Preserve respectively to the east, south, and west. The Northern State Parkway, meanwhile, borders the preserve to the north, completing the rough rectangle of the haunted woods where people believe the ghost of Mary dwells.

Some people might prefer the word "stews" over "dwells," for Mary's ghost is believed to be hateful of humans. Folks say she is angry about her death and seeks revenge. However, if we accept the legends of Mary burning down the school, it's probably safe to say she was hateful of humans long before she was put to death. Her act of killing children by burning down a school or a hospital is a clear indication of her predisposition.

Mary is said by some people to haunt Mt. Misery Road just as fervently as she haunts Sweet Hollow Road, maybe even more so.

In a story posted on *Newsday.com* in mid-October, 2008, the unnamed writer draws attention to the fact that Mt. Misery Road was named a "Street of Fear" by FearNet.com, a network for horror enthusiasts. The short *Newsday.com* story about FearNet's choice to select Mt. Misery Road as one of the ten creepiest roads in America, said:

> "During the day, Mount Misery Road is a nice, leisurely country drive. At night, the narrow road with no streetlights, surrounded by woods with houses set back far from the road, can create a surreal feeling, especially if you've read the next paragraph:
>
> Among the lore here are several "Mary's Grave" stories and the twice-burned-down mental hospitals. The first hospital burned down and hundreds of patients and employees didn't escape in time, they say. The second, which opened 15 years later, lasted just five months before a female patient burned it down. They say the sound and smell of these events echoes and lingers in the surrounding woods. Then there's the "Lady in White," who appears in front of cars and then disappears just as fast."

We find generally the same stories about Sweet Hollow Road also circulating about Mt. Misery Road. No doubt, this is because both roads border the same woods where Mary is said to have burned down the building and then been unceremoniously buried in disgrace after being executed in a fire or hanged in the woods for her black sins.

Thus, the ghost haunts both roads.

Regardless of what road the legends are attached to — Sweet Hollow Road or Mt. Misery Road — the facts stated in both legends are false, according to Huntington Town authorities.

Though the name "Mt. Misery" conjures images from horror movies, Robert Hughes, Huntington Town Historian, pointed out that the name has more to do with practical matters than ghosts

or ghouls. He said the name "Mt. Misery" comes from the hill being difficult for travelers to get horse-drawn wagons up it back when the road was unpaved. The locals found the task of going up the hill such drudgery they named it Mt. Misery.

Hughes suggested anyone with any sense would not have built a hospital or school in the woods atop a treacherous hill gotten to by means of an unpaved road that would have been difficult or impossible for people and horses to climb in rain and snowstorms. After all, schools and hospitals are intended to be easy to reach so people can utilize them.

In the case of a hospital, for example, people's lives are at stake. Reaching a hospital quickly in an emergency is vital. In addition, hospital employees, doctors, vendors, and visiting family members also require safe roads in order to reach the hospital, too.

In the case of a school, no mothers or fathers in their right minds are going to send their children to lessons at a school where their kids could get swept away in muddy torrents of storm water gushing down a hill, or where the kids could drown in deep puddles created by heavy rains.

The fact is there was never a school or a hospital on Mt. Misery Road back in the olden days when Mary was said to have burned the building down.

End of story.

Acknowledging this fact necessitates dismissing the "burning building" legends associated with Mary. For many people, this is easier said than done.

Regardless of how often we tell people at our lectures that the legends of Mary of Sweet Hollow Road are false, the stories still circulate as though they are fact. We have even seen people coming up to us after lectures in which we said the legends are false, only to ask if the legends are true. When it comes to the Mary legends, it's as though people can't hear the truth, as though they want to believe the lure.

Writers of books that include stories about Sweet Hollow Road also perpetuate these legends. While these writers do not claim

the legends are true, the mere telling of the stories in a way that does not dismiss them as false lends credibility to the stories, obviously equating the tales with truth in some readers' minds.

People like scary legends about the places they live. Some things you just can't change.

Legend of Mary in Head of Harbor

One other well-known place in Suffolk County where many people believe a killer known as *Hatchet Mary* lived and was buried is in Head of Harbor. This is a small north shore hamlet at the edge of Stony Brook Harbor.

The "Mary legend" of Head of Harbor is very similar to some of the Mary legends that are known from Sweet Hollow. It's probably the second best known ghost story of Mary on Long Island. Because of its striking similarity to the legend of Mary's grave at Sweet Hollow, we thought it should be discussed briefly for contrast purposes and because people often ask us about this site, claiming there is little information to be had about it.

Head of Harbor is the site where many ghost story enthusiasts claim a woman named Mary chopped her husband to pieces with a hatchet inside their home on a hill. Legend says when she died she was buried in a graveyard near the harbor.

Other stories of Mary of Head of Harbor say she was killed by a jealous lover or by her husband. Again, the legends depend on with whom you speak. We've heard people claim that Mary's ghost can be seen on full moon nights or when car headlights are shined on her gravesite.

But in reality, the brown-colored stone walls at the site where people claim Mary is buried are not parts of a grave nor part of a graveyard. An objective investigator will note that the two walls were obviously erected as part of a small structure that housed a well and piping for a well. A tiny spring bubbles out of the ground at this site and a sign erected by Suffolk County warns people not to drink the water from the spring.

Head of Harbor. Legend claims this is the place where Mary was buried. *Photo by The Paranormal Adventurers.*

How legends of the ghost of Mary sprung out of this place is unknown, but like the water from the spring, people should not swallow the story.

More than likely, people see mists rise from the ground in the area of the spring on account of the warmer moisture meeting colder air, and in the headlights the mists may look like ghosts. It's hard to say why this legend in Head of Harbor persists. Whether or not Mary's grave is located in a spot further back in the thick woods of the marshland behind the stone walls is impossible to say, for trees grow in such tight clusters there that getting though the terrain is impossible. In addition, even if the trees were removed, it's possible there would be pockets of marshland likened to quicksand in this area. Hiking in this marshland could prove fatal.

Locals we interviewed in Head of Harbor told us they have never seen a ghost in the area, and all but one person said they

are not familiar with the house where Mary supposedly lived and killed her husband. In addition, they said they know nothing about a local woman buried alongside the harbor.

One local man we interviewed, who said he had never seen a ghost there, showed us the house on a hill where he said Mary killed her husband. But the house looked too new to us to have been around for the many decades that the legends of Mary's grave have been around.

Visitors can reach the supposed site of Mary's grave in Head of Harbor by means of Harbor Road, which can be found intersecting from the north side of Main Street in the Stony Brook Village park area. Harbor Road winds around as it leads up and down hills before reaching a tiny park against the harbor, with the reputed site of Mary's grave only a stone's throw away.

For some time visitors to Head of Harbor have claimed Mary's grave is located in marshland situated to the east beside the little park on the water. Ghost hunters who go to this place typically park their vehicles in the tiny park's stalls, because there is no shoulder on Harbor Road, and they walk a few hundred feet back up the road to a place on the north side of the road where two walls of stones are located. It can be dangerous walking there because the road is narrow, so be careful. Use flashlights at night to warn oncoming cars. Dangers are multiplied by going there at night. The safest bet is to go to this site only during daylight.

In contrast to Head of Harbor on the north shore, Sweet Hollow, located more or less in central Long Island, is the site of a ghost several people we've spoken to swear they've seen in one form or another. Moreover, we've **seen** such apparitions. The contrast between the two places is sharp. Witness testimonies, as well as what we and other paranormal investigators have experienced on the road and in the woods of Sweet Hollow, supports the conclusion that Sweet Hollow is haunted. However, nobody we've ever met had an experience with a ghost at Head of Harbor.

Though we have met people who claimed to have seen the ghost of Mary on *the haunted mile* or in Melville Cemetery, Diane and I have never seen her, despite countless visits to the road, cemetery, and the woods.

A male ghost did smack my hand three times in the course of one night, float over and around us, and yell at me, but it was not Mary. I'll get back to this paranormal incident later.

Alas, we have never seen Mary's grave in the Melville Cemetery where it's said she was buried. The reason we never found her grave in the Melville Cemetery is because it doesn't exist.

Of course, this is not to say the ghost of *Mary* does not exist. Or better stated: This is not to say a ghost people *call* Mary does not exist. To the contrary, personal experiences, and some physical and photographic evidence, support the notion that such a ghost does exist.

‡‡‡‡‡‡‡‡‡

Melville Cemetery

We suspect *convenience* is the chief reason that Melville Cemetery on Sweet Hollow Road is popularly believed to host the grave of a ghost named Mary, and that *convenience* is similarly behind the reason why so many people are so quick to delude themselves into believing Mary's ghost releases from a gravesite there nightly.

After all, as long as visitors are in their vehicles, Melville Cemetery can be visited without much difficulty in any kind of weather. That's convenience!

In this respect, the Melville Cemetery is like a drive-through creep show with visitors not even needing to get out of their cars to look for ghosts. They just have to peer through the car's windows.

Melville Cemetery on Sweet Hollow Road. Many people believe the ghost of Mary dwells here. But more likely, her ghost dwells in an old graveyard in the woods on Mt. Misery. *Photo by The Paranormal Adventurers.*

Most people who we see visit the cemetery to search for ghosts do not bring cameras or other investigative tools because they are not ghost investigators; they are ghost enthusiasts and are hoping to see a ghost on their fun adventure. Who can blame them? It's fun to look for ghosts. Diane and I refer to this approach as "ghost hunting lite." There is certainly nothing wrong with this method of ghost hunting. After all, everyone has a right to ghost hunt on a level of their own choosing.

Ghost investigators, in contrast, approach a reputed haunted place with tools and discriminating minds in hopes of gathering evidence and documenting their findings for or against the place being haunted. They take a more forensic approach to an environment, searching for signs that could dispel reasons to believe a place is haunted, or evidence that spirits dwell there.

Such lax requirements for ghost enthusiasts who do not approach a haunted place in a methodical manner play favorably to carloads of loud visitors who we have often noticed enjoy such comforts as eating McDonald's food, listening to rap music, and exchanging excited ghost stories, half in curses, all from the

warm, dry comfort of their cars — what amounts to a floating viewing room, living rooms on wheels. In this case the graveyard is like watching a movie on a panoramic screen; it's like a big video game.

At night, of course, visiting Melville Cemetery is more difficult because the black wrought iron gates are locked and vehicles cannot enter the grounds. This requires amateur ghost hunters who are determined to find ghosts in the supposedly haunted graveyard to park some distance away, walk to the cemetery, and illegally circumvent the fence to enter the grounds.

Amateurs tend to not want to do any hard work when ghost hunting, so Melville Cemetery is a perfect place for them to go to imagine ghosts and have fun. Some of these kinds of empty ghost experiences at Melville Cemetery are posted in videos on the Internet at YouTube under a search of Sweet Hollow Road.

It seems that by night, in particular, paranormal enthusiasts who visit Melville Cemetery more often than not let their imaginations take over. They tend to interpret every wind as the breath of Mary on their faces, hear every noise as her groans and curses, and see every shadow as her ghost flying through the cemetery.

No doubt, many people who claim to see things in the cemetery at night are telling the truth. But what they see might be exaggerated by their imaginations and their desire to see *something*.

"Matrixing" is a term widely used by ghost investigators to explain piecing together faces and bodies from features of the environment, such as making faces out of clouds or people out of shadows in graveyards. Matrixing produces ghosts where none exist. It's likely many people could be accused of matrixing while visiting Melville Cemetery.

Conveniently, escape to the relative safety of civilization is easy for those who end up scared inside Melville Cemetery. Once outside the imposing gates many people feel they are back on safe and familiar ground, and are no longer as afraid as they were in

the graveyard. They are now quick to excitedly swap their stories about what they've seen and experienced. We know this from having observed many people during our Paranormal Undercover study in which we watched from the cover of darkness the whacky and ridiculous things people do when they visit Sweet Hollow Road at night in search of ghosts.

We have interviewed many of these people. Most of them are high school and college kids out for a night of fun. They are not serious ghost investigators.

One night, we observed some kids climbing the tall wrought iron gate of Melville Cemetery in order to get inside the graveyard. They put themselves in jeopardy of getting hurt. Unbeknownst to them, all they had to do was walk around the gate to an opening twenty feet away in order to enter the grounds. At the north side of the gate between a brick column and a tree is a large opening people can easily walk through. But these kids didn't know it. Yet when they came out of the graveyard and we interviewed them they said they found ghosts.

Hmm.

We've witnessed many people illegally entering Melville Cemetery at night to get inside to catch a glimpse of the ghost, "Mary." This was especially true during many dark nights of our Paranormal Undercover study.

As mentioned, the study was intended to find out what people did on the road at night when they didn't know they were being observed. Sometimes we hid in bushes or clusters of trees with our video camera set on infrared and aimed at sites we knew were of interest to visitors searching for ghosts.

Sometimes we asked these people questions when they came out of the cemetery. To this day, nobody has been able to tell us with any authority out of *which* grave Mary rises; and nobody we ever met under these circumstances has ever photographed or caught Mary rising out of a grave on video, though we have personally met and also heard of many people who claimed to have seen "something" in the cemetery. Most people report a

According to legend, only the name Mary appears on Mary's Grave.
Courtesy of Karen Isaksen.

fleeting shadow or a figure flying across the grounds.

You might recall an earlier discussion with Mike Salvia of Old Bethpage, who had experiences outside the gates of Melville Cemetery one summer night. When we recorded him speaking about that night for our DVD, "The Ghosts of Sweet Hollow Road," he said that he and his female friend "felt watched" while they were photographing the Melville Cemetery from outside the gates. It was during this time and under these conditions that he photographed the images of milky white forms that he believes were manifestations of apparitions. *(Visit our website to view the photographs or buy the DVD.)*

Of this night, Salvia recalled, "The weather was clear. It was just a perfect, beautiful night. There was no fog, mist, rain, or anything."

So while there is no historic evidence to suggest Mary dwells as a ghost in Melville Cemetery, many people suggest their personal experiences there support the notion that there are ghosts in the cemetery. Salvia's experiences at the graveyard led him to believe there is spirit activity there.

At this point, we must warn anybody with notions of illegally entering Melville Cemetery at night that any number of unwanted consequences could occur — ranging from getting hurt to getting arrested. If you believe the stories of Mary and

that spirits can follow people home from cemeteries, then you should consider, too, that an angry spirit could follow you home...maybe even Mary!

If you want to see the graves in the cemetery, go during the day when the cemetery is open. But you won't find Mary's grave in the Melville Cemetery during the day either because it doesn't exist.

The Lady in White

Blending with the legend of Mary is the famous legend of the "Lady in White." This ghost story of the *Haunted Mile* is popular with visitors to Sweet Hollow Road because many people have either seen her or experienced her ghost in some other way.

Supposedly, the specter floats down Sweet Hollow Road in the middle of the night. Some say you can hear her weeping and calling out for help.

The ghost of Mary is often seen at night on Sweet Hollow Road.
Courtesy of Karen Isaksen.

According to some versions of the legend, the Lady in White is a ghost still wearing her wedding dress, for she was a young bride killed in a car accident on her wedding night on Sweet Hollow Road. This legend is also attached to Mt. Misery Road where people report the *Lady* has also been seen.

Many legends of the Lady in White contradict the wedding night story: some legends say an angry lover killed her while others say her husband killed her. These legends start to blend with the legends so often heard from other hamlets pertaining to Mary.

While events in the stories about the Lady in White are the creations of imaginations and are not based in fact, eyewitness accounts of the Lady are real.

Barbara Loiko of Farmingdale, said she saw the ghost of the Lady in White many times in the thirty years she worked at the now defunct Meyer's Farm on nearby Old Country Road in Melville.

"She was all white and dressed like a Gibson Girl in turn of the century clothing," said Loiko. "I saw her on Sweet Hollow Road. She just sort of floated."

Loiko described the ghost as radiating her own white light. She said the Lady was easy to see without the aid of headlights because of this. She added that there was no particular time of day or night when she saw the ghost, but most times there was very little traffic in the area and the road was "quiet."

Frank Greco of Franklin Square, on the other hand, told us his eyewitness account for our DVD, "The Ghosts of Sweet Hollow Road." Greco said he witnessed a female friend being pulled backwards along the ground into the woods by her hair by an unseen woman who only the girl could see. An invisible entity was trying to claim the girl for its own, he said.

Greco reported the incident began when the girl tripped and fell to the ground while visiting the area. When the girl tried to get up she found she could not stand because the ghost of a witch had a clump of her hair. The girl's locks were wrapped tightly around the witch's wretched fingers. The witch yanked the girl to what the entity apparently intended to be the girl's death in the woods.

During this time only the girl could see the witch and she was reportedly a dreadful hag.

Seeking a tool to cut the girl's hair loose from the entity, Greco and the girl's other friends ran to their cars and dug up a pair of scissors and then ran back to the girl and cut her hair so they could get her away from the invisible fiend, said Greco.

"We didn't know what to do," explained Greco as he stood on Sweet Hollow Road while we videotaped his story. "We were screaming and crying and everything!"

Greco claimed the girl "was bald" after the incident.

Mary appears on Sweet Hollow Road as the illuminated form of a woman.
Courtesy of Karen Isaksen.

Diane and I have interviewed many other people who claimed to have seen apparitions and strange light anomalies along the *Haunted Mile*. Telling these people the legends of Sweet Hollow Road are false doesn't convince them, for they *know* what they've seen and felt and nobody can tell them differently. Greco and Loiko would have to be added to this growing group of believers.

We understand the way people feel when they relate their personal stories of what they witnessed on Sweet Hollow Road. Diane and I have *witnessed* ghosts. Nobody could ever dissuade us from what we know to be real and true. We would never try to tell other people that their experiences were not real, either.

Perhaps the legends of Sweet Hollow Road were born of actual events whose stories grew evermore legendary and pat as the years progressed. Or maybe the legends and stories have been a means for people to explain the sightings of ghosts and paranormal events on the road throughout the years.

According to Huntington Town authorities, a woman was never killed on her wedding night on Sweet Hollow Road. Additionally, we could find nothing printed in books, newspapers, or vertical files that said there was such a death. Nor could we find evidence that a woman was killed in or around the nature preserve by an angry lover or husband.

We do know of at least one murder connected to Sweet Hollow Road, though we do not attach any ghosts to this murder.

In June 1976, the nude and rope-bound body of thirteen-year-old murder victim Kathy Woods was found four days after she went missing, wrapped in white canvas, discovered by a family of bicyclists only twenty feet into the woods on Sweet Hollow Road at a location far north of the nature preserve. Woods had been abducted from a road in Dix Hills and had been sexually abused. Her killer was never found.

One reason the murderer might have picked Sweet Hollow Road to dump the girl's body in the dead of night "is because you can see a car's headlights coming from a half-mile away," said Tom Philbin, an author who investigated the Woods case at the time it occurred.

"It's the creepiest road I've ever been on," said Philbin, a Centerport resident and co-author of *Killer Book of True Crimes*, published in 2007. "It's just pitch black there at night! Really creepy!"

The area where Kathy Woods' body was found was so far north of the Haunted Mile that her murder plays no role in either the legends of the road or our investigations.

The History of Sweet Hollow

Sweet Hollow was the early name for today's hamlet of Melville in Suffolk County. The hamlet is located more or less in central Long Island amid the hills that ride the spine of the Ronkonkoma Moraine, a line of hills left over by the ice age.

It's possible the hamlet was called Sweet Hollow because of the sweet smell given off by trailing arbutus flowers in the spring. Laurie Farber, a teacher and environmentalist who knows the area well, brought this flower to the attention of Suffolk County Legislature back in the mid-1970s when she was instrumental in nudging the county into acquiring the then privately owned land for public usage. Partly due to Faber's and some other people's efforts, the county bought the 174 acres of land that today composes the West Hills Nature Preserve. The same flowers still populate the woods and give off their sweet aroma up till June, Farber noted.

Some say the name "Sweet Hollow" came from the wild honey that could be gotten in the woods in the old days. Others say the name it has to do with an overturned wagon filled with molasses.

Farther back in time, before the hamlet of Melville was even called Sweet Hollow, the area was known as Samuel Ketcham's Valley. The Ketchams were one of the earliest families of settlers in the area.

Today the forgotten Ketcham Family Burying Ground is lost deep in the woods on the southeastern slope of Mt. Misery Road in the West Hills Nature Preserve. Few visitors pay respects to the memories of the thirty-one people buried in the tiny graveyard.

There are no cleared trails cutting through the woods to the Ketcham Cemetery. The graveyard, too, is overgrown. It's so cluttered with thorny vines, poison ivy, and wasp and animal nests that it's difficult to find or to move around in without getting hurt.

The tiny Ketcham Family Burying Ground is lost deep in the woods on the southeastern slope of Mt. Misery. *Photo by The Paranormal Adventurers.*

When we visited the graveyard one warm September day we uncovered only about a dozen or so of the thirty-one graves which the Town of Huntington says it has photo-documented at the site. A sign fastened to a chain-link fence around the graveyard announces to visitors that the parcel is a Huntington Town historic cemetery.

Diane and I, and a handful of other intrepid hikers, led by Laurie Farber, director of the Starflower Experience, a children's environmental learning group, uncovered two graves at the Ketcham Family Burying Ground with the name "MARY" etched into the weathered limestone. On one of the stones the name was especially pronounced at the top of the slap. The stone belonged to Mary Ketcham. She died in 1811 at age twenty-five. She was married to Timothy Ketcham.

We wondered if Mary Ketcham's two hundred-year-old stone could have contributed to the legends of *Mary* of the area. In particular we wondered if the *Mary's Grave* legend was born of this gravestone. The legend says Mary's "grave" bears only the name "MARY" on it and no last name, birth or death dates.

Could Mary Ketcham's gravestone been the model that loosely shaped the legend of "Mary's Grave" in Sweet Hollow?

Mary Ketcham's grave. Did this two-hundred year old gravestone contribute to the legends of Mary of Sweet Hollow Road? *Photo by The Paranormal Adventurers.*

Certainly, wide-eyed children sitting around a blazing bonfire on a farm on a windy Halloween night in the hollow in the mid 1800s might have referred to the Ketcham graveyard as a haunted place in the woods, with stories of ghosts rising out of the graves on full moon nights. Maybe Mary Ketcham's grave was a reference point for these stories. Possibly, it was Mary's grave out of which people had seen spirits rising. Or more likely, perhaps people attached sightings of a female ghost in white in the hollow to Mary Ketcham's grave because she died so young.

Samuel Ketcham's Valley was located at the northeastern corner of the Bethpage Purchase.

The Bethpage Purchase is a term referring to a fifteen-square-mile area of land that Thomas Powell, a devout Quaker, bought from three tribes of Indians in 1695. Powell settled with his family in a place he named "Bethpage" in the heart of the land he bought from the Indians.

Though history books tell us the New World offered religious freedom for those who were persecuted in other countries for their beliefs, the Quakers, who were pacifists and non-conformists, found much intolerance in America before and after the United States declared its independence from England in 1776.

According to Huntington Town Historian Robert Hughes, Thomas Powell lived in Huntington before he packed up his family and moved to Bethpage. In Huntington he "found he could not support the Congregational Church" so he found a place to live where he could express his own religion, said Hughes.

To this end, a meetinghouse for the Quakers was built in Bethpage. It's a place known today as The Old Quaker Meeting House. In front of the meetinghouse is The Old Quaker Burying Ground. Diane and I have investigated this graveyard on many occasions and determined that it is paranormally active. Many people were buried there without gravestones. The results of our investigations at this cemetery will be presented in a future book.

Diane and I are currently investigating aspects of a theory we call "The Black Hat Theory," which examines a Quaker connection to Sweet Hollow. This connection might be the source of a tragedy we think could be at the heart of the hauntings on the road. The theory is discussed at more length in our DVD "The Ghosts of Sweet Hollow Road."

If and when our Black Hat Theory is worked out so that it makes sense — and strong evidence is gathered to support the theory — we will publish a book devoted entirely to Sweet Hollow and its hauntings. In the meantime, visit our website regularly to keep abreast with developments on this topic.

Other Legends & More Strangeness

The Black Dog

Some of the other false legends of Sweet Hollow Road include a story about a black dog that walks on its hind legs and is a portent of doom. Some people say it has glowing red eyes.

According to Rosemary Ellen Guiley's *Encyclopedia of Ghosts and Spirits*, this legend dates back hundreds of years to British folklore and the legends of the "black shuck," a "spectral dog."

The story of the black dog may have been brought to Long Island when English settlers transplanted from Salem, Massachusetts to Sweet Hollow in the late 1600s, looking for a new place to farm.

Salem was the home of the witch trials of 1692. The witch trials were responsible for the hanging of nineteen men and women and the death of another man by "pressing" with crushing heavy weights.

The people of Salem were notoriously superstitious. It's likely the newcomers to Sweet Hollow brought with them the legend of the black dog when they arrived—and that the story stuck through the generations.

Sweet Hollow Road's legend of the Black Dog of Death. *Courtesy of Karen Isaksen.*

One September night, in our audience at the Commack Branch of the Smithtown Library, a woman told us that she was on a beach when a black dog appeared to her and her children. The black dog walked right passed all the other people on the beach straight for them, looking only at them, even while it was still far away. When the strange black dog arrived at their blanket and opened its mouth, they saw the animal was missing the same teeth the woman's aunt had been missing from her mouth before she died.

"We think that dog was her and she came back to tell us she loves us," the lady said in summary.

Another woman who told me her story some years ago said one night while she was ill with cancer and couldn,t sleep, she looked out her bedroom window on the second floor of her home and saw a black dog standing still as a rock outside on the dark street. The dog was staring up at her. The black dog had been staring at the window from the street even before the woman pulled the curtain aside and saw it. She said she felt that the black dog was there to deliver a message.

"It sat there for the longest time," she said. She always felt it was a spirit letting her know she was going to be all right. Her cancer went into remission and last I heard of her she was still alive and healthy, many years after the dog appeared to her.

The Spectral Cop

There is also a legend about a police officer who appears on Sweet Hollow Road in the dead of night and signals drivers for help only to reveal vacant eyes and blood dripping all over his shoulders and chest. When he turns to vanish into the night, drivers see the back of his head is missing.

The cop who stops people in the dead of night only to reveal the back of his head is missing. *Courtesy of Karen Isaksen.*

While we never met anybody who ever experienced this ghost cop on Sweet Hollow Road first-hand, a young man in one of our audiences said he had a friend many years earlier when he was in the sixth grade who told him that he and his mother were pulled over by a cop on Sweet Hollow Road and when the cop turned around, the back of his head was missing.

The boy's experience is an exact match to the legend of the ghost cop. We suspect the sixth grader made up the story. Nonetheless, it's the only time we ever heard someone tell us that they knew somebody who actually saw the ghost cop of Sweet Hollow Road.

Whether or not this experience truly happened to the young man's friend and his mother will probably never be known. The young man who told us the story refused to tell us the boy's name so we could contact him. We wanted to ask the man's friend and his mother questions about the story so we could determine its authenticity.

The fact is a police officer was never killed on Sweet Hollow Road, according to Huntington Town authorities.

Just like the legend of the suicide teens, there is no information to be had from libraries or newspapers about the police officer because the murder of a cop on Sweet Hollow Road never happened.

This is not to say people haven't seen the ghost of a man in uniform on the road in the dead of night.

Indeed, we have posted on our website in the "Photographs" section for this book Photograph 1A of an apparition we shot in the daylight on Sweet Hollow Road that matches this billing. The apparition appears to be wearing a coat with a wide collar that might be of military style, such as a coat worn by an officer in the Civil War or perhaps a police officer in the early twentieth century.

West Hills Nature Preserve

In the area of strangeness, odd human behaviors in the nature preserve runs a close second to ghosts. You might be surprised to know there is a perverse sexual dynamic going on in the West Hills Nature Preserve.

This sexual energy was first brought to our attention on a warm, sunny spring morning around Easter 2005 when Diane and I met a very nice woman at the entrance to the nature preserve and with whom we struck up a conversation.

The woman explained to us that she had never seen ghosts in the woods, but that she had discovered a "secret spot" where a man and a woman had been exchanging gifts for some time, and in at least one case, one of the two people left an explicit pornographic photograph for the other to find.

The woman explained to us that she had alerted authorities to this pornographic exchange because she often brings children hiking in the woods as part of her duties as a teacher. She was particularly fearful children might discover the smut.

Specifically, the woman said she once discovered a photograph of a man's penis and genitals. She found it under a rock at the

secret spot located beside a tree amid the white pines not far into the preserve. She showed us the exact location of the secret spot in the woods. On the very day we met her, she said she had found a yellow Easter egg containing a gaudy fake gold pendant (see photos on our website). I donned latex gloves and examined the pendant. There was nothing outstanding about it.

On later investigations Diane and I discovered other items left by the two mystery people at the secret spot. Once a slip of paper simply read, "We have the potential." We left this item where we found it under the rock.

Another time we found a book of matches from a restaurant.

In the days following Halloween 2007 we found near this secret spot pumpkin shells, some with the wax from spent candles sitting in the bottom of the shells. It appeared as if a group of people had visited the woods, sat on the logs of fallen trees, and had a story time or a prayer time without disturbing the environment with a fire. Perhaps witches had met there and honored the season with prayer and gentle candlelight. Whoever had visited the spot was obviously respectful of the woods and the sanctity of the earth because no garbage was left behind and the pumpkin shells were not smashed.

I have been out in woods with witches on a few occasions for stories I have written for newspapers. I came to know Pagans as sincere, caring humans who honor the earth and the universe at large. I always regarded my experiences with the witches I met and wrote about to be valuable eye-openers. Witchcraft is not about riding broomsticks and casting evil spells. Rather, it's about a person's personal relationship with nature.

The pumpkin shells could also have been used to hold candles that gently illuminated the night for lovers who met and spread out a blanket over the soft pine needles to make love. We will probably never know.

Perhaps the most bizarre human encounter we experienced in the woods took place one cool spring day when a man with a red shirt bolted into the woods only to hide amongst the trees to spy on us.

The odd stranger had noisily entered the woods after slamming his car door loudly shut where he parked, right outside the entrance to the woods of the nature preserve. He then darted into the woods at full steam and ran past me.

Thinking I was bird-watching with my camera equipment, the man said, "Good day for bird watching!" He was out of breath. He continued running awkwardly onward, deeper into the woods. He was not wearing sneakers, but shoes. Instead of running sweats or shorts, he was wearing expensive black slacks. The pieces of the puzzle didn't add up.

Only seconds later, as we watched him running up the trail, the man came to an abrupt halt, turned sharply into the trees, and vanished into the dense growth. A moment later he showed up hiding behind some trees so he could watch us. While he appeared to make an effort to actually hide, it was such an insincere effort that we couldn't help but spot him immediately. Not only did we have him in our sights the entire time, we even caught him hiding on video. You can watch this video on our website.

Diane waved the man off as just another piece of the plentiful evidence attesting to the strangeness of Sweet Hollow's woods, and she went off to do some independent meditation among the nearby trees, careful to remain within earshot of both me and another male investigator with us at the time.

Several moments later Diane returned with an incredulous expression on her face. "Oh, my god!" she exclaimed. "Everywhere I go!" She meant that the man was hiding behind trees and watching her everywhere she went in the woods.

Though she had never been in danger because I and the other investigator were nearby to protect her, the experience shook Diane up to the reality that perverts could wander the woods. This is something to watch out for at West Hills Nature Preserve, especially for female ghost investigators. It's best to always be partnered with somebody when in the woods of Sweet Hollow.

The Spirits

One summer day in 2004 Diane and I were photographing Sweet Hollow Road when we both felt a strange feeling in our chests. It's the feeling we get when the spirits are around. As ghost investigators we learned early on to recognize this feeling as a sign from the "other side." It means the spirits are around us.

The day was sunny. The temperature hovered around eighty degrees. Only the gentlest of summer breezes blew. In truth, the breeze was so slight one might suggest there wasn't any breeze at all.

I had my camera aimed up the road. Diane was beside me studying the area that I was photographing.

"Do you feel it?" she suddenly asked.

I always marveled at our connection with the spirits in this way. Diane and I always experience the exact same heavy feeling at the exact same time when the spirits are calling. When it first started happening on investigations we wondered whether or not this feeling was universal. But we found out from others who were with us on subsequent investigations that they do not feel it. So, the calling card from beyond was more intended for Diane and me.

This always made sense to us because we have long believed we were invited to become ghost hunters by ghosts themselves. It's as if they chose us, rather than us choosing them.

"Yes, I feel the heaviness," I replied, gazing up the road looking for ghosts. "I can taste the alkaline."

I had long ago learned to pay attention to this feeling and strange taste.

The feeling is one of heaviness. A taste comes along with it. For me, it's the taste of alkaline. The foul taste always reminds me of my summer stay on a ranch in Wyoming when I was twenty-years-old. The well water on the ranch was filled with alkaline and tasted just like Alka-Seltzer, the popular gas remedy.

160

Perhaps for that reason, I always associated the taste with illness, specifically fever.

Though the feeling is one of heaviness, there is an inexplicable emptiness that accompanies it. Neither of us welcomes this feeling. It is foul and we worry about what it means. For example, is this how death feels? Does it mean the spirits are touching us at this very minute, or are they inside us?

Nobody really understands how ghosts work. We don't understand how they have the physical ability to touch us, such as on the shoulder or on top of our heads. Scientists haven't found the mechanisms spirits use to get inside people and make us feel things or enter our dreams. On the surface it appears that it would be impossible for spirits to enter people, but the reality is that many people believe in possession and in mediums that speak in the voices of dead people.

We have seen people overcome by spirits, and it's not pretty. For instance, we saw Maureen Wood, the well-known medium from New England Ghost Project and radio show host of "Ghost Chronicles" (1490 WCCM), overtaken by spirits while doing a séance at the haunted Houghton mansion in North Adams, Massachusetts. Maureen appeared to be ill and in pain. What's worse, she was not in control of herself. The spirit *controlled* her. She spoke in voices that were not her own.

The heavy feeling we experience when the spirits are around us never lasts long. Most times it lasts only five or ten seconds. Some ghost hunters we know, however, have reported to us that they grew sick while on Sweet Hollow Road and the illness lasted weeks, and in some cases, months. They point to Sweet Hollow Road as the source of their illnesses. While most of these people will not state as fact that the spirits of the road were ultimately responsible for their sickness, the links among the spirits, the road, and their illnesses are usually suspected as the cause.

Well known ghost investigator and author Matt Haas grew sick one day while on an investigation with a paranormal research team at Sweet Hollow Road. He called it a "depression" that at

least one other team member also came down with. Haas said the illness lasted weeks. Several other people grew sick during that investigation. In one case, Haas had to help a sick woman out of the woods — "out of harms way," as he called it.

So it was while the feelings of the spirits were upon me and Diane on this particular day while photographing the road, and while we were searching for other signs of the spirits, that a whirlwind suddenly swept by us like a small tornado and picked up dirt, sand, and leaves from off the road and spun it all together like a top before our eyes. The narrow vortex stood about twelve feet high.

Then just as quickly, the dirt, sand, and leaves fell back to the pavement and the tornado was gone. Instantly, all was normal again.

"They're back!" Diane said.

We looked at each other with acknowledgement that the tiny windstorm we just witnessed should never have happened. We knew that what we had just witnessed was a paranormal event.

It was very much like the time I was fifteen and with five other people at a creek in Oceanside, Long Island, when, in broad daylight, my friends and I heard feet pounding the ground. We turned around to the sounds only to see the dust rising right behind us in a big sandy lot. There was nobody there. But *something* had pounded the ground there!

Moments later we heard the feet pounding the ground again, but this time the feet ran through the sandy lot and down a tiny sand hill right beside us. Not only was dust rising into the air in the middle of the lot behind us, but dust had also been stirred up and was now rising on the hill upon which sat. We had heard the feet pounding the earth as they ran down the hill and to a path right in the area where we were sitting. The entity not only stomped the earth with its ghostly feet, but ran right beside us so we would know that it was there!

We stared with wide eyes and open mouths.

Then moments later — as we were discussing this mystery, frantically searching for its meaning, for its source — it happened again.

This time the dust rose into the air from the middle of the lot, down the hill right beside us, and hundreds of feet down a narrow dusty path running alongside the creek. At the end of the line of rising dust floated a ghost. It hovered in the air above the creek. It was a white ghost. It had to be eight feet tall. I could see its long arms and legs, its shoulders and waist, its hands and feet, its head.

Its body shifted like it was made of cigarette smoke or water mist. But all the while it maintained the shape of a human. People of Oceanside who live along the creek are so familiar with this lanky ghost that they even have a name for it: *Sasquatch*.

I quickly snapped off a round of photographs following the little tornado on Sweet Hollow Road that Diane and I witnessed many years after I saw the ghost at the creek in Oceanside. When we arrived back at our studio and examined the photos we saw that the first photograph in the series following the paranormal event contained faces. This particular photograph was the one shot immediately after the "vortex."

The faces of three women and one man appear in this photograph. People in our audiences raise their hands to indicate they see these faces when we ask them if they do.

One face in particular stands out. It's the face of a woman that can only be described as scowling at us. She does not appear happy. I often think of her as Mary. *(To view this photograph, visit our website.)*

In the photograph, the face of the woman who I refer to as "Mary" looks as if it's either dirty or burned, with lines on her face etched with darkness, as if the creases and lines had captured and held dirt or perhaps soot from a fire. Her eyes are accusatory; her lips appear dry and set in an angry expression.

After we saw the face in the picture, we wondered if this was the Mary people had been seeing over the generations on Sweet Hollow Road and Mt. Misery Road.

The faces of the other two women in the photograph, and the face of the man above Mary, took a second place to Mary's tortured face.

‡‡‡‡‡‡‡‡‡‡

Diane and I had an interaction with the ghosts on the road one dark night in 2007. At least one of these spirits was the shade of a male who struck me.

We were photographing on the road outside the entrance of West Hills Nature Preserve when the sickly feeling that alerts us to spirit activity revisited us. Unlike the time we photographed "Mary," we were now equipped with an 8 mega pixel Sony digital camera with a Carl Zeiss lens. In contrast, we photographed the "Ladies of Sweet Hollow Road" in 2005 with a basic Polaroid digital camera. In 2004, when we bought the Polaroid, digital cameras had just recently come on the market and were not as advanced as they are today. We call the Sony DSCF828 digital camera we purchased in 2005 "The Dark Angel" because of its ability to capture ghostly images.

The pitch-black darkness of quiet Sweet Hollow Road on this night was frightening because it was so dense. There are no lights on the road in front of the nature preserve. There was just the strip of road. The woods were like tall walls towering over us. At times it felt like the woods were closing in on us.

I was holding the Dark Angel. My habit is always to have the camera's strap around my neck so that if I drop the expensive camera it will not fall to the ground and break. Also, I typically hold the camera up with my left hand and squeeze off shots by pushing the shutter button on top of the camera with the index finger of my right hand.

"Do you *feel* it?" Diane asked. She was referring to the "heavy" feeling the spirits induce.

"I do," I said, and I took a deep breath to try to exhale the feeling out, for it's most unpleasant.

I stepped to the edge of the road to the entrance to the nature preserve, but still standing on the pavement of the road. As I exhaled, I felt my left hand suddenly smacked. I lost grip of the camera and it toppled against my chest.

Something slapped my hand! I remember the feeling of the hand that hit me. It was cold and not human.

It happened so quickly that I was momentarily stunned and confused by what I had just experienced. At times like these the events are so unnatural that processing information is not instantaneous. Piecing together the pieces of the paranormal puzzle takes a few seconds.

Nonetheless, the hair on the back of my neck felt as if fingers were rushing through it, but it was just my nerves and adrenaline surging. The pumping of my heart swelled in my ears and the sides of my face crept with a spider web tingle from blood shooting wildly in my veins. In those few seconds, as I searched for meaning of what had just happened, I held my ground, not moving in any direction — not because I'm brave, but because I didn't know what was happening!

My left hand was now holding the camera again. The sickly heavy feeling was still upon me. I searched the night.

Then it happened again.

A hand, cold and hard, hit my left hand with such force that I dropped the camera. Again, the Dark Angel smacked up against my chest. If I didn't have the camera strap around my neck, the camera would have smashed to pieces on the hard black pavement.

"Over here!" I called to Diane.

My voice trembled because my body was on high alert. My adrenaline was reacting to a code red emergency: a ghost was haunting me! An intelligent entity was interacting with me!

The oldest part of the human brain, the hypothalamus — the part that signals "fight or flight" — was instructing my body to react as if a predator of the jungle was upon me, the way our ancestors reacted thousands of years ago when saber tooth tigers still prowled the night.

I felt a cold wind rush the left side of my face as I again took charge of my camera. This is the moment that every ghost hunter dreams of, but which few of us are prepared for because one's reactions to such an experience cannot be planned.

In these seconds — which had now accumulated into a minute — I had been so preoccupied with my own experience that I had forgotten about Diane and what she may have been experiencing.

"It's right behind me!" she called suddenly. She sounded wired, tense, thrilled.

I turned and saw her step quickly forward with her left shoulder dunking in such a way that it seemed she was trying to get away from something. She pulled quickly from where she was standing as if a ghoul was about to grab her shoulder from behind.

"Take a picture!" she ordered.

Ghostly mists form around authors Joseph Flammer and Diane Hill in front of the West Hills Nature Preserve one haunted night.
Photo by The Paranormal Adventurers.

Coming to my senses, I quickly snapped off a photo of Diane.

It is my habit not to look into the viewfinder when I snap night shots. Instead, I have learned it's more valuable to look *above* the camera to see the images illuminated by the flash. Very often in haunted places I see the images of the spirits looming as mists. In older times, these mists might have been called "ectoplasm." Most people refer to these mists as *ghosts*. Casper the Friendly Ghost is an excellent example of what people have experienced as ghosts over the millennia. Casper is white, misty, and not bound by gravity.

My eyes were trained on the blackness of the night in the area behind Diane when I pressed the shutter down.

The camera's flash filled the long black valley of the haunted road.

In the light I saw the white blob of a creature standing behind Diane. It had the shape of an animal that I could not identify from the brief appearance in the brilliant light of the flash, but I remember it seemed to be hovering above the road. Later when

The face of a ghostly creature with a long snout stalks author Diane Hill from behind as she photographs the haunted night on Sweet Hollow Road.
Photo by The Paranormal Adventurers.

I reviewed the photo I saw the creature's long snout, almost terrestrial-like, with two eyes peering at me as I snapped the picture.

In a second photo that I quickly shot my eyes caught the images of several more of these white blobs, these ghostly forms, in other areas on the road, past the creature looming behind Diane. One in particular filled the camera's viewfinder.

I was stunned. I was about to tell Diane what I had just seen in the viewfinder after taking the photograph. But before I could speak I felt a hand on my left shoulder.

I tore myself away from the space I was standing as Diane had done only a minute earlier when the ghost was behind her. My heart was pounding like jungle drums in my ears.

As I jerked away, I saw a white form moving above me in the darkness. My eyes could see this shape without the aid of a light because it had a certain quality of its own that

The misty form of a ghost changing shape fills the camera's lens. But in the light of the camera's flash, author Joseph Flammer could see other forms hovering around co-author Diane Hill. *Photo by The Paranormal Adventurers.*

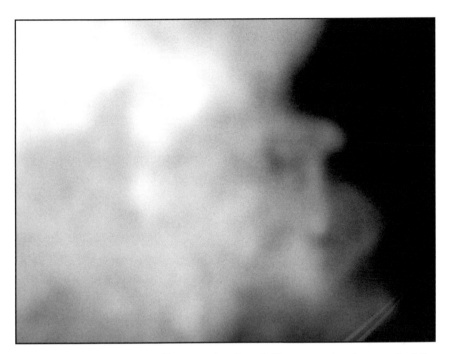

Notice the face in the mist smiling at author Joseph Flammer as he photographed the ghosts haunting him, slapping his hand, and shouting at him on Sweet Hollow Road. *Photo by The Paranormal Adventurers.*

illuminated its shape. The illumination was far dimmer than any kind of light that one might imagine; yet the image of the entity was brighter than something that simply had a milky white form. Whatever lighted it, the result was the ghost was more pronounced in the immediate area around me in the darkness than anything else. Yet I still could not make out what kind of figure it was, whether it was merely a cloud of mist or an apparition with the shape of a human or an animal. I snapped off a shot.

In only seconds the form drifted slowly away from me. I watched it move like a slow cloud away from me and vanish.

I squeezed off another shot.

Chills were flying up and down my spine. Ghosts were everywhere! The empty feeling of illness, of alkaline in my mouth, was present and strong. Paranormal cobwebs dragged across my

During an hour of a haunting on Sweet Hollow Road mists formed, broke up, formed again and came alive with ghosts. *Photo by The Paranormal Adventurers.*

face and hands. I felt as if everywhere around me was a presence observing me, ready to touch me.

Diane yelled, "Over there!"

I turned to her.

"It's right there!" She pointed.

Even in the darkness I could see a white shape standing beside Diane. It had that same luminescent quality. But she was not aware of this ghost beside her. In fact, at that instant, she was pointing away from herself to an area at the edge of the road!

I squeezed the camera and saw at least three white blobs in the flash. Three ghosts – three classic Casper the Friendly Ghost forms – looming before us on the road, giving us their full paranormal attention. Only I can't say they were as friendly as Casper!

I stepped closer to the edge of the road to take another photo. Just then my hand was slapped again and the gruff voice of a man shouted, "No!"

The image of a ghost that slapped author Joseph Flammer's hand three times on Sweet Hollow Road, each time knocking the camera out of his hand. "No!" the gruff voice of a man also shouted at him. *Photo by The Paranormal Adventurers.*

The camera tumbled out of my hand and against my chest.

"Stop!" I shouted. My shout was involuntary, a reaction, not a request. I'm certain that at that moment my hair was standing straight up for every system in my whole body surged in reaction to the unnaturalness of the frightening event. I breathed quickly as I looked all around for its next appearance.

I snapped off a photo and glancing at the viewfinder I saw that I had captured a large purple orb and streaks of white mist in the photograph. The mists seemed to follow the orb. A rectangular purple orb appeared in the left hand corner of the viewfinder. I knew the forms were spirit manifestations.

Now a white form that I could see only vaguely appeared looming over me. It was just a few feet from my face. The form was long and appeared as dense as a large white bundle of tightly

A rectangle and a large purple orb with trailing mists appear in a photograph. The author, Joseph Flammer, had expected to photograph the mists that loomed in front of him, but instead, he photographed these orbs, giving some credence to the opinion that orbs can be paranormal anomalies.
Photo by The Paranormal Adventurers.

packed cotton. It was like a thick white cloud in which someone was wrapped inside. It was floating above me. I felt its cold air sweep across my cheeks as I backed away from it. I felt as if it had a personality, intelligence, and that it was watching me, amused by my reactions.

I backed up a few feet and remained as still as I could. The truth is I was so awestruck I was petrified. The ghost drew closer to my face again and hovered over me.

"Who are you?" I shouted.

The white figure did not move, but now I noticed it wavered like a flag in the air above me, though there was no wind.

I had seen this wavering before. The ghost I had seen when I was fifteen at the creek in Oceanside with five other people wavered in the air like a flag in its own wind. It shimmered the way a heat mirage on a road wavers in the distance on a hot day in the desert. I'll never forget the way the creek ghost moved and shifted position as we watched it. Some of the kids were crying because the event was too strange and overwhelming. We knew this happening would change our lives. There was no wind that day, either.

I waited for the spirit hovering above me on Sweet Hollow Road to answer, but no answer came. I backed up slowly, turning to see what was behind me. Diane and I were now standing next to each other searching the night. I snapped off a last shot.

It was then I noticed the dim sheen of a car's headlights coming down the road from the direction of overpass. It was still far off in its approach to the overpass. When I next turned back to the ghost, I saw nothing in the air before me.

Ten seconds later, the car that was coming from the north finally passed through the tunnel of the overpass with its high beams aimed in our direction; the headlights revealed nothing out of the ordinary on the road or at the sides of the road.

The sickly feeling had simultaneously evaporated. The ghosts were gone.

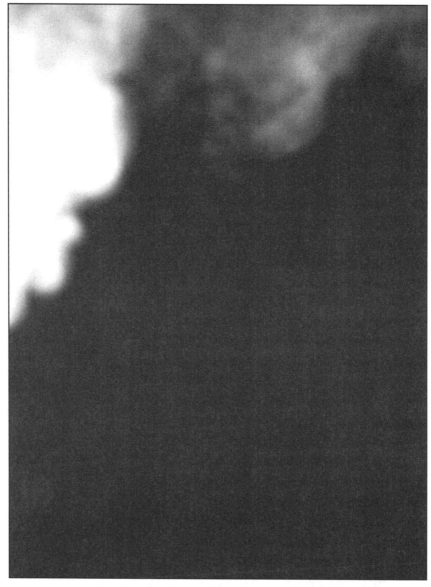

A face wrapped in mist stares down at author Joseph Flammer during a haunting on Sweet Hollow Road. *Photo by The Paranormal Adventurers.*

Always the professional, Diane rushed to my SUV to get our video camera and tripod. Though we would shoot video of the road for an hour following, we caught nothing unusual, and our photographs went back to just ordinary shots of a dark night on a lonely country road.

The memories will always be with us.

It wasn't until we got back to the studio that night and examined the photographs that we notice the towering image of a tall man with sideburns hovering in a dense black cloud on the side of the road. There is only one photograph of this man. This image of the tall man is absent in all our other photos taken with the same camera of the same area at approximately the same time. *(This photograph and the photos of the mists that interacted with us that night can be viewed on our website.)*

It was on this very night as we were shooting video that a carload of high school kids pulled over in front of the nature

Outlined by red is the image of a tall man standing in the trees at the edge of the road. This was shot on the night authors Joseph Flammer and Diane Hill were haunted for an hour on Sweet Hollow Road. *Photo by The Paranormal Adventurers.*

preserve. The driver killed the engine. Out of the car poured five high school kids. We were parked across the street on a dirt patch people use as a parking area.

The teens were itching to ask us questions, no doubt, because in the headlights when they pulled up they saw Diane standing behind the video camera set on a tripod as well as a big black camera around my neck. People often stop and ask us questions about the ghosts of Sweet Hollow Road as we're investigating, usually ending the night for us because most times these people want to stick around and watch us.

These five teens, however, as tempted as they surely were, did not ask us any questions. They proceeded into the woods. I didn't see them holding any camera equipment, but I did see one of the teens flick on a small flashlight as they entered the nature preserve. We watched the light go up the trail in the woods and heard their voices discussing what they were seeing as the light vanished into the dense trees.

"Should we say something?" I asked Diane.

"Say what? That we were haunted by ghosts tonight?" she asked. "They'll think we're nuts!"

"Yeah, you've got a point," I responded.

We waited for the kids to start screaming, but no screams came.

About ten minutes later, however, we heard the thumps of their feet hitting the ground in heavy footfalls. The teens were talking loudly. Then we spotted the light of the small flashlight the boys were using to light their way in the woods reappear on the trail as they quickly exited the trees.

I shone my flashlight on them from across the road. Their faces were drained of blood. "Did you experience anything?" I asked.

The five teens all began muttering excitedly at the same time. One teen's experience stuck out from the others and I focused on him.

"What happened?" I asked him.

"We were walking through the woods when all of a sudden something hit my hand," he exclaimed. "It was trying to knock the flashlight out of my hand! We got out of there fast!"

I trained a flashlight on this young man's wan face. He seemed somewhat dazed. I wanted to interview him at length about this. I wanted to ask his name and record his story on video, but I suspected he was under eighteen and that would make him a minor.

"How old are you?" I asked.

"Seventeen," he said.

I could not interview him.

"What was it?" he demanded. "What hit me?"

I thought of the photo of Mary we had taken years earlier with our simple Polaroid camera following the vortex that appeared to Diane and me on Sweet Hollow Road. "A ghost," I said. "It could be Mary. It could be somebody else." I thought of the man's voice that shouted "No!" at me that very night. "It could have been a male ghost. I had my hand slapped tonight, too."

"Yeah, well, I don't want anything to do with this place," the kid said. "I had enough."

The boys got back in the car and left Sweet Hollow. We always hoped they didn't bring any spirits home with them. If they thought they had a bad time in the woods, wait till the spirit wakes them up in the middle of the night at home!

Investigations

We have been investigating Sweet Hollow Road as *The Paranormal Adventurers* since 2005, but we were investigating the road for several years before we gave ourselves a name and started writing articles for national magazines such as *Ghost!* and *Haunted Times*, and freelancing for Long Island newspapers such as *Dan's Papers* in the Hamptons and *The Long Island Advance* in Patchogue. It wasn't until 2006 that we began speaking publicly about ghosts at Long Island libraries and before community and historical groups.

During these many years we have tried a number of investigative techniques to detect and reach the spirits of the road and the woods. Some of the techniques we employed might be labeled "clumsy" and "low tech" by sophisticated ghost investigators with their arsenals of expensive equipment.

Sometimes we employed a large wall clock and a large clock-like thermometer that we set side-by-side in front of the video camera at a known cold spot in the woods in an effort to see if the temperature fluctuated; the clock was intended to reveal to us at a glance the exact durations of the fluctuations. Since much of our work is presented to audiences in lectures, we also wanted the audience members to see on the big screen what we saw while in the woods. But nothing ever happened. We recorded many dull hours of a clock, thermometer, and some other items that never moved. Sometimes you win, sometimes you loose.

If suddenly the clock started spinning backwards and the thermometer dropped twenty degrees in three seconds it would have been an amazing piece of evidence to show people. In the ghost-hunting field, you learn what works as you go along.

Incidentally, regarding the study of cold spots, we did discover that although we could feel cold spots in the woods on our flesh, there was no correspondence to temperature. In other words, the cold spot did not differ in temperature from the ambient temperature of the air in the woods, though the cold spot clearly *felt* much cooler than other areas of the woods. There are several known cold spots in and around the woods of the nature preserve. We're not going to tell you where they are; this is something you should discover for yourself as you get to know the woods and the road.

Some of our techniques, on the other hand, might have been responsible for producing results. Spirits are not about coming back to the world of the living so they can be photographed or recorded on video. They choose when and where they will appear. They have their own agendas.

Imprints, on the other hand, often called "residuals" are imprints of images or sounds on the environment. Since the imprints have no intelligence, they also have no choice. An imprint is like a tape in a VCR that plays over and over again without any apparent rhyme or reason. In this case, the ghost may actually be a vision instead of a being from the other side. The theory about imprints is that a traumatic event was recorded, or "imprinted," on the environment, possibly at the spot where the event took place. There is no intelligent entity behind the imprint.

Expensive equipment is very useful in detecting differences in the environment that might indicate something unusual — something paranormal — roaming around a given area. Ghost investigators use electromagnetic field detectors to find variations in electrical fields in an environment. Investigators often use sophisticated thermometers, thermal recorders, and a host of other tools in an effort to narrow down areas of a house or other types of sites wherein ghost activity reportedly occurs. These investigators are skeptics who have to be convinced by the evidence they collect that something paranormal is going on in the location they study, or they wave their hands at the place and say it's not haunted because they have no proof of it.

Diane and I have a great respect for their approach. Unlike the unruly teenagers who run amuck on Sweet Hollow Road looking for ghosts — and usually see them behind every rock and tree — these investigators seek to employ scientific method to their approach, as best they can. Most ghost hunting groups on Long Island pride themselves in the strict methodology they claim to follow during investigations.

Diane and I don't need to be convinced that ghosts exist. We've both seen them. We're already convinced. We seek to delve deeper into the mystery. Our goal is always to first confirm their existence in a place by experiencing their presence, chiefly by feeling them around and photographing their manifestations. Then, we try to communicate with them. It's our hope that one day we will turn

a key that allows us to have an actual conversation with a spirit to find out what it's like on the other side.

Thus, we are in search of ghosts to ultimately communicate with them, rather than piecing together evidence to support notions that spirit activity is present in a given location. However, narrowing down the area where a spirit might dwell could accelerate opportunities for direct communication.

I saw three ghosts in my day. My first ghost sighting was in Oceanside when I was fifteen and with five other people. I saw the ghostly Casper-like mages on Sweet Hollow Road the night I had my hand slapped three separate times and heard a man yell "No!" as I was about to take a photograph. And I saw a black **shadow person** walking across a field on the former Bell farm in Adams, Tennessee, where the infamous Bell Witch Ghost terrorized the Bell family for years before outright killing John Bell by poisoning him with an unknown black liquid.

Diane and I spent four days investigating the tiny town of Adams, Tennessee. The ghost I saw there was walking briskly through the tall grass in a meadow. It was tall and blacker than black. It was the color black of black steamers hung around a room for a Halloween party. Diane and I were in the company of Pat Fitzhugh, the author of books that are the last word about the Bell Witch. John Bell's murder at the hand of the Bell Witch ghost is the only documented case of a ghost killing a human being. The murder is officially recognized by the state of Tennessee. A plaque erected by the state on a cabin owned by the Bell family states so. Pat Fitzhugh is a decendant of the Bell family through his mother. He believes he's had experiences with the spirit of the Bell Witch. One experience is that the ghost toyed with him when it appeared as a rabbit.

The chief tool Diane and I use when investigating Sweet Hollow Road or any place is our own bodies. We have had numerous personal experiences in which we felt touched, or a brisk cold air rush past us, or heard murmurings, voices, music, laughter, screams, or saw strange images that were not actual ghosts, but

were ghostly, such as orbs seen with our own eyes. We have seen ghostly activity, too, such as things moving.

As we discussed earlier, we have learned to acknowledge the particularly odd sensation in our chests that signals when the spirits are around. This sensation feels heavy. It lasts for only seconds, but we have come to recognize the feeling as a calling card from *beyond*. We don't know how the spirits could trigger this or by what mechanism they can enter a person or sap healthiness from a human body like they do electricity from batteries. We're just glad they don't stay in our bodies!

Very early on we decided we would not investigate the portion of Sweet Hollow Road north of the Overpass because we did not in any way want to disturb the privacy and tranquility of the residents in areas beyond the nature preserve.

Though there is much road to study beyond the overpass — over another mile of it heading north towards Jericho Turnpike (Route 25) — we determined that enough paranormal activity took place along the *Haunted Mile* to keep us occupied for a long time to come. So deciding not to venture in that direction narrowed down our field of study to a place that is still enormous, but that over time we have been getting more familiar and about which we are growing more knowledgeable.

We sometimes wonder if our decision to focus on the area of the nature preserve had a favorable impact on the results we experienced and continue to experience along the *Haunted Mile*. Whether or not the spirits grew more accustomed to us and decided to communicate with us because of it, or whether it was just luck that we were around when the spirits wanted to show themselves, or if the *Haunted Mile* is simply the most haunted area of the road and we just happened to be there when it was active, or if the nature preserve is the only haunted area of the long road, we will probably never know.

Nonetheless, we have photographed the kind of ghostly images along the Haunted Mile that people call apparitions. Others might call them **shadow people**. Whatever you want to

call these images is fine with us, as long as you see what the possibilities photographing similar images at Sweet Hollow Road are for you.

‡‡‡‡‡‡‡‡‡‡

The most startling photograph we've taken on the road was shot right in front of the West Hills Nature Preserve, which is clearly marked by signage erected at the entrance to the woods. The nature preserve should not be confused with the county park with picnic tables and a baseball field that is a half-mile north of the overpass in the direction of Jericho Turnpike.

The spirits in the woods of the nature preserve have always made us feel as if we were being watched, as though we were amongst others whom we could not see.

Once, while investigating the woods during broad daylight, another investigator and I heard a woman scream loudly somewhere amid the trees nearby. This took place while Diane was studying a part of the woods in an area not immediately near us and in the opposite direction from where we heard the scream originate. It was a brief, shrill, frightening scream, as though the woman was terribly scared. It sounded authentic.

I was shooting video at that moment. Without delay I turned the video camera to the area of thick woods from whence the scream had come and quickly moved in that direction. But seconds later, when I got to the place where the woman who screamed should have been standing, there was nobody there. I was momentarily stunned because I had expected to see a human being. There was no place for anyone to have escaped! But instead, I had to confront the fact that once again I was in the land of ghosts, a haunted place where unexpected and strange events take place.

As a ghost investigator in the woods of Sweet Hollow, you, too, must expect these kinds of strange happenings to occur. You have to go with the flow of these experiences if you are to get to

know the spirits of Sweet Hollow. You may want to ask yourself first why you even want to investigate the place for ghosts, and then ask yourself if you really want to commit yourself to the pursuit of ghosts in these woods and on Sweet Hollow Road, so when the strange stuff begins happening — the hauntings, that is — you understand why it is worth the fear.

One day in October 2008 filmmaker Christopher Garetano from Northport and a second cameraman were recording Diane and me in the woods of Sweet Hollow for an upcoming Halloween segment on CottonMouth.TV (http://cottonmouth.tv). When we were finished recording inside the woods, we stepped out onto the pavement of Sweet Hollow Road near our cars. A flood of water from up the road near the overpass streamed down towards us. It gushed down the slight incline of the road and ran right in front of our feet in the area where we were standing and where our cars were parked. Within seconds, the dirt patch beside our cars was saturated by a wide puddle that we had to jump over to get to our car doors.

It was not raining. I remember telling Garetano and his cameraman that this was the kind of strange thing that often happens on Sweet Hollow Road — not a *bad* thing, just strange.

We took our cars and drove up to Gwynne Road where Garetano wanted to shoot us in the last of the day's light talking about the legends of the road. When we got there we saw the cause of the flooding was an open fire hydrant that was shooting water in a wide, forceful geyser. Gravity was pulling the water downhill toward Sweet Hollow Road. From the corner of Gwynne Road the water flowed down Sweet Hollow Road to the entrance of the nature preserve.

Garetano was recording us when a car from the Melville Fire Department arrived at the gushing hydrant. A fireman used a large wrench to close up the water valve, stopping the geyser. It took him a couple of minutes to completely stop the gushing water. We rushed to the fireman and I asked him if this kind of problem happens often on Sweet Hollow Road.

"Yes," said the fireman. "All the time... Kids!"

The strange thing is, we didn't see or hear any kids in the area just prior to the water rushing down the road at us. The water could not have taken more than five minutes to travel from the hydrant to our cars on at the entrance to the nature preserve. But during those five minutes, while we were standing beside our cars and talking, there weren't any teenagers around that we noticed. If there had been, what kick would they have gotten from opening up a fire hydrant in the woods on a Sunday afternoon? And how would they have done that? A very large wrench must be used to open the valve. Why would they chance being arrested for a joke nobody would witness or even know about? After all, it wasn't like there was any audience there to appreciate the prank!

The spirits of Sweet Hollow Road can disarm a person easily and steal one's self-assurance. Sometimes you will feel like a passenger on a train that is moving quickly and gradually coming off the tracks. You will want to hold onto the sides of the seat and steer the train back on track. But you are not in charge. You have very little control over what happens. It all takes place too quickly to redirect events. We don't understand why the spirits on the road behave like this — why they shake up our world to the point that we are unsure of the truth of reality.

Moreover, we never understood why ghosts in general don't lend themselves to being seated and interviewed so we know why they are haunting us. Rather, they show themselves the way a slight of hand magician shows his tricks. It seems almost playful on the part of the paranormal. But it's not funny to us.

Be centered when you approach Sweet Hollow Road and don't forget to tell the spirits to stay where they are when you leave, or you might have problems at home. We can't tell you any specifics problems you might encounter. It seems personal experiences vary widely.

And please don't blame us for what you draw into your life by going to Sweet Hollow Road. After all, we are *The Paranormal Adventurers* and we do this because we *are* ghost hunters.

You have to decide on your own level of commitment and you must be prepared not to back down when the time of fear comes so that you can document what takes place. You'll understand better what we mean when the time arrives.

Good luck.

‡‡‡‡‡‡‡‡‡‡

View Photographs Online

Now let's look at some photographs. In order to view the photographs you must visit our website, www.paranormaladventurers.com, and follow the links.

Photograph 1

In this we believe we have photographed the apparitions of an old man with a drooping mustache sitting on the ground (middle left) and a woman standing over him holding her hand to her mouth as if taken aback by something she sees. In the same photograph we also see the apparition of a man with wavy brown hair and a mustache. He is standing on the right side of the photograph with a patch of light underneath him. The apparition is wearing a coat with a collar. He is looking directly at the camera. Photograph 1A is a close-up of this apparition.

Photograph 1A

Here, we caught multiple images of apparitions. These images are isolated and blown-up on the computer screen to make them easier to see. This is true of the apparition of the man on the right side of Photograph 1 that is isolated in Photograph 1A.

Rarely are so many images caught in one photograph as we have captured in Photograph 1. However, we have experienced this in our photography many times on Sweet Hollow Road. It seems as though when one apparition appears, there are usually

others to be found within the same photograph. We don't know the reason for this. Some people have suggested that a "portal" exists at Sweet Hollow Road that allows spirits from "the other side" to enter our world. It's an interesting suggestion, but there is no way we could verify this.

In the case of Photograph 1, we believe we are catching a scene in progress more so than mere individual apparitions who just happen to be in the same spot and eager to show themselves to our camera. The question is what is going on in this scene? Are we witnessing an event, a tragedy? Why does the woman in Photograph 1 look so stunned? Why does she hold her hand to her mouth as if appalled by something she is seeing?

Now let's examine Photograph 1 in depth.

Photograph 1B

This is the section of Photograph 1 that shows the profile of a woman holding her mouth. Sitting on the ground to the left of the woman is a man with a drooping white mustache, white hair and a black hat on his head. The man is looking at the camera as we photograph him.

The shadow woman appears to be holding her mouth aghast at what she sees. She holds the heel of the palm of her hand against her mouth. You can see her fingers before face, the black indent of her eye, her high cheekbone, her forehead, and the bun in her hair. The bun is held together by a light colored band wrapped around the middle.

The woman appears to be wearing a Victorian-styled blouse with a high neck and three-quarter length sleeves. The flesh of her forearm near the wrist is uncovered. If you follow the arm down from her hand you can see the point of her elbow and from there you can follow the fold of her arm leading back up to her shoulder. Like the apparition of the man in Photograph 1A, the woman's body starts to fade as it goes from the waist to the legs.

She seems shaken by something she is witnessing. What does the shadow woman see that upsets her so?

This photograph has the added bizarre dimension of hosting other faces. Some of these faces are located to the left of the man, also with black hats on their heads. Another face with a black hat on its head is wedged right between the woman and the man who is sitting on the ground (see Photograph IC). The face between them appears male, very dark, and cartoon-like, though while staring at the photo to see this face, you might notice other faces pop up that superimpose over the first face you were examining. Incidentally, this cartoon-like feature is another trait of many of the photographs taken on Sweet Hollow Road. But for us, the oddity of suddenly seeing other faces superimposed over the original face being studied is a phenomenon that occurs exclusively with photographs taken at Sweet Hollow Road. If you photograph there, be prepared to see this phenomenon when you get home and study your own photos. The spirits show up in multitude in many photographs, and they overlap and superimpose over each others' faces.

Some of the faces you may see in the photograph Diane and I might have never even noticed. It's not uncommon for people in our audiences to point out new faces in our photos even after the many hours we spent studying them.

Sometimes the faces of shades show up in large number and it's easy to drift from one face to another as you study the photograph. Some ghost hunters might suggest such areas that reveal multitudes of faces of the dead are "portals" to the *other side*. We are not prepared to support such a far reaching hypothesis as to suggest Sweet Hollow Road is a portal to the other side because to verify the truth of the hypothesis would require exhaustive experimentation, and in the end, it is unlikely we would ever get an answer as to whether such a thing exists. Besides, we're busy enough just trying to get a basic understanding of what is going on at the site. However, it's a great topic for others to pursue now that they know where to look for paranormal activity.

There is an additional bizarre feature in Photograph 1. It changes as you look at it. Let's witness this change in the photograph.

To see the change look at the woman holding her hand to her mouth in Photograph 1. If you look at her long enough you will see her change into a young girl who is standing in profile. The girl is perhaps five or six years of age.

To see the woman change into the girl look at the black indent of the woman's eye in Photograph 1. Now see the eye turn into the black area that is the space between the young girl's shoulder and chin. You will see the young girl if you follow the features of the face up to the girl's mouth and nose, eye, forehead and hair. Like the older woman, the girl's hair is also bound in a bun and held together by a lighter colored band wrapped around the bun.

The girl is in a tense stance. Her legs are poised as if she is reacting to something menacing, with her left arm out as if to ward off danger.

Some people in our audiences believe the girl is sitting on a bicycle. They point out the wheels.

You might want study this picture to see the woman change into a girl. The change does occur if you study the photo. Thousands of people in our audiences at hundreds of presentations have seen it.

In the very same photograph is yet another clear figure, though, again, you might see more faces in the photograph in addition to the ones we will be pointing out to you:

On the right side of the original photograph, just over a light patch on the road, is the apparition of a man (see Photograph 1A. He has wavy brown hair and a mustache. He appears to be wearing a coat of some kind that has a wide collar. People have suggested he's a soldier although there's not enough detail to tell who he might have been. Nonetheless, there he is, and he is looking directly at the camera. This phenomenon is repeated by almost all of the apparitions of Sweet Hollow Road. It seems that shades see us though we can't see them while we're photographing.

Now you may say, "These images aren't ghosts! These shades don't have the exact likeness of humans!" We'd say,

"Correct, they don't. That's why they are shadow people, shades of people, not the actual people. Only people are people. These are the shades — the shadows, the apparitions — of the people they once were.

These images abound at Sweet Hollow Road. They are showing themselves to us. We believe they are telling us a story. They are pieces of a mysterious puzzle. We believe someday when we put the many pieces together we will solve the puzzle and have a single, cohesive story that makes historical sense.

Photograph 2

In this photo, we believe we caught the faces of three shadow women on Sweet Hollow Road. We had to lighten the photograph to see the details of their faces more clearly.

While the woman's face on the right side of the photograph is the clearest of the three, it's the partial face of the woman in the middle that is most intriguing to us because we can see only her nostril, nose, upturned mouth and perhaps the deep empty socket of her left eye. The rest of the face is missing. This problem of the missing features begs the questions: How do shades materialize for the camera and manipulate light? Was she just materializing or was she dematerializing? A photo snapped only seconds later does not contain these faces. Where did they go and why did they show themselves to our camera?

Further Study

For an in-depth examination of the paranormal activity on the road, you should buy *The Paranormal Adventurers'* DVD, "The Ghosts of Sweet Hollow Road," completed in the fall of 2009. The DVD is available for purchase at www.paranormaladventurers.com.

Bibliography

Lakeview Cemetery

Field, Van R. *Wrecks and Rescues on Long Island*. Patchogue, New York: Searles Graphics, Inc., 1997.

"Ghost Chase in a Graveyard." *Brooklyn Daily Eagle*, March 3, 1895.

"Patchogue's Cemetery Ghost." *Brooklyn Daily Eagle*, February 28, 1895.

"The Ghost Has No Head." *Brooklyn Daily Eagle*, March 1, 1895.

Machpelah Cemetery

Brandon, Ruth. *The Life and Many Deaths of Harry Houdini*. New York, New York: Random House, Inc., 1976.

"Broken Wand Ceremony." The International Brotherhood of Magicians, http://www.magician.org/portal/node/311. Accessed November 23, 2007.

Gibson, Walter B. *The Original Houdini Scrapbook*. New York, New York: Sterling Publishing Company, Inc., 1976.

Kalush, William and Larry Sloman. *The Secret Life of Houdini: The Making of American's First Superhero*. New York, New York: Atria Books, 2006.

Pine Hollow Cemetery

Evans, Martin C. "The House on the Hill." http://www.Newsday.com.

Hammond, John E., Historian. *Historic Cemeteries of Oyster Bay: A Guide to Their Locations and Sources of Transcription Information.* Oyster Bay, New York: Town of Oyster Bay Historian's Office, 2007.

Sweet Hollow Road

Cagney, Oakley, W. *The Heritage of Long Island.* Port Washington, New York: Kennikat Press, 1970.

Gabriel, Ralph Henry. *The Evolution of Long Island.* New Haven, Connecticut: Yale University Press, 1934.

"Historical Disclosure." *The Long Islander*, September 15, 1876.

Jackson, Birdsall. *Stories of Old Long Island.* Rockville Centre, New York: Paumanok, Press, 1921.

Merritt, Jesse. *The Huntington Historical Society.* Long Island, New York: The Huntington Historical Society, 1953.

Naylor, Natalie A. "The American Revolution Beyond New York City: 1763-1787." *The Long Island Historical Journal* (Fall/Spring 2006): 155-158.

Index